FULL CIRCLE

To NANCY SEILER A FELLOW LION WHO KNOWS WHAT "IT" IS ALL ABOUT !

Jack Oliver

An Autobiography By

John "Jack" W. Oliver, Jr.
COLONEL USAF RET.

ISBN: 1466323760
ISBN-13: 9781466323766

FULL CIRCLE

An Autobiography By

John "Jack" W. Oliver, Jr.
COLONEL USAF RET.

CONTENTS

PREFACE

Never in my wildest imagination would I have ever thought that I would end up in the military services as a Regular Army Officer and a triple-rated Flying Officer—Pilot, Celestial Navigator, and Bombardier—with a secondary degree in Astronomy from Louisiana State University.

I was born and raised to be a Texas A&M Aggie, a county "Ag" agent, or a High School "Ag" teacher, running my own family farm near my home town. Someone planned my life otherwise!

How could a country boy from Belton, Texas, end up as a Command Pilot, having first flown as a crewmember on a B-24 bomber, and then piloted P-51 Fighters, P-80 Jets, DC-3 transports three years in South America, and B-29 Bombers? In addition, how likely was it that that same young aviator was to be one of the first Satellite Master Controllers, Satellite Test Directors and Satellite Operations Officers at Vandenberg AFB; then be Commander of the Kaena Point Satellite Tracking Station in Hawaii; further, following nine years in Satellites, be assigned as a full Colonel, Chief of Staff of SAMSO, the only US Armed Forces and Air Force Space and Missiles Command located in Los Angeles, California?

For that matter, how probable was it that I would someday return to Texas and my GI farm, later sell it, only to eventually gather up all of my dad's 192 acres, make it home once again, and live out my life on that old 1874 Oliver Farm?

I would be remiss if I did not give credit where credit is due. True, my dad encouraged me, but the person that was by my side every day of all those years—since January of 1944—was my wonderfully understanding and considerate wife. Yes, credit goes to Miriam Garrick Oliver, my wife of sixty-seven years, from Charleston, South Carolina! Following those WWII combat days when we lost one hundred percent of our men and B-24 Bombers in six months—when replacements came fast or we couldn't have flown our missions—I was lucky to be able to come home after my 53rd Combat Mission and my second Purple Heart. Thank you, Miriam, for always being there for me with a tender and loving heart!

ACKNOWLEDGMENTS

The author owes a great deal of thanks and deep appreciation to the following persons whose dedicated efforts made the publication of my *Full Circle* story possible:

Durwood "DJ" Heinrich, Ph. D., Consultant, Author, Pilot, and my friend.

Gloria Ramos, Belton, Texas, for her untiring efforts in the initial preparation of this manuscript for publication.

Miriam Oliver, my wife, my son Robert Oliver, and my family, whose warm understanding and encouragement made this work possible.

(1)

THE OLIVER FAMILY

My grandfather, William Henry Harrison Oliver, was born in Clarke County, Georgia, November 20, 1841. His father was Francis Hewitt Oliver, a veteran of the War of 1812, who was the son of John Oliver who served in the North Carolina Militia in the war of The American Revolution. He served three short-term enlistments. He was eighteen years old and was living at his father's home in Oxford, Mississippi, Granville County. They had moved from Chesterfield County, Virginia, at some earlier date. His pension papers state that he was born on January 12, 1762, in Chesterfield County, Virginia. He came from the stock of John Oliver (1609) and Peter Oliver and his descendants of the later 1600s and 1700s.

The Francis Hewitt Oliver family of Clarke County, Georgia, moved to Warrior Stand, Alabama, where the father died in 1849. About 1850, the widow and her ten children—eight sons and two daughters—moved to Neshoba County, Mississippi, where her brother, Robert Love, had purchased a farm for her.

Each of the eight sons was called up to serve in the Confederate Army. The second son died of measles in camp, and the youngest son—only eighteen years old—was never issued a gun or a uniform because the war came to an end.

My grandfather served in Company E, 40th Mississippi Infantry, as a Private. He enlisted in May 1862 and served at Corinth, Mississippi, in the siege of Vicksburg and at Chattanooga, Tennessee. During the fighting at the siege of Vicksburg, the oldest brother, Richard Lewelling Oliver, was shot through the body. Because of the blockade of the southern ports, medicines were either in short supply or non-existent. Fortunately his brothers were able to pool their gold coins and pay the forty dollars needed for an ounce of iodine. He survived the war and lived another twenty years when he died of a stroke.

My grandfather was captured at Vicksburg in 1863 and subsequently paroled—possibly *exchanged?* His service ended in 1865 and he walked home from northern Georgia. My grandmother mentioned several times that his shoes did not have lining, nor did they fit very well. He was forced to cut the shoes off his feet in strips where blisters had formed.

My grandfather was the seventh of eight sons and eight in the line of ten children. He was never a sturdy youngster, and in the 1850s he spent a lot of time at the home of his uncle, Judge James Robert Shelburne Love. His uncle's wife had died, but the house Negroes cared for him even when the Judge was absent. After the war ended, he continued to live at the home of his mother much of the time. He operated a country store in her home and planted a ten-acre apple tree orchard. When forty years old, he married our mother, Eunice Walters, age twenty, and lived on a farm a few miles away. At the farm, he planted peaches, a few early apples, raspberries—both red and black— and quince. My aunts recall riding on a wagonload of apples picked up in grandmother's orchard and dried by being spread out on the roofs at home.

My grandfather died at Laurel in Jones County, Mississippi, on July 5, 1901, after having multiple strokes. Our mother took his body back to be buried at the Pine Grove Cemetery in Neshoba County where his mother, two brothers, and his first son, Robert, were buried.

His mother—our great grandmother—died at age eighty-eight, leaving the farm to a bachelor son and the two unmarried daughters, Adeline and Louisiana, who had cared for her in her old age. When the son died in February 1901, the farm was sold, and the two sisters moved to the home of Ben Oliver in Bell County where they lived out their days. His two brothers, Ben and Gus, had no children and sent for their sister-in-law Eunice and family after their brother's death. Their incomes were small, but the brothers' offer gave them a chance, and after two years they were self-supporting.

My father, John Walthall Oliver Sr., was born in Laurel, Mississippi, in 1899. When his father died in 1901, his mother and the family moved to Texas. Two of William's brothers had gone to Texas after the Civil War. Ben ran wagon teams from Austin to Waco, and Gus ran oxen teams from the Brazos landing northwest of Houston to Waco.

As mentioned earlier, Ben and Gus insisted that their sister-in-law, Eunice Walters Oliver, bring her seven children to Texas to live with them, which she did in 1901. They settled on Ben's farm, five miles east of Belton, Texas, and Ben built them a home. Gus owned a farm next door.

Ben and Gus owned and operated some six hundred acres of prime farm land in the middle of Three Forks Community. The community had no stores but did boast a thriving church and community school of seven grades. High-schoolers went to Belton, five miles away. The Oliver uncles insisted that the children get a good education. All of the girls became community teachers;

and one, Sadie, became a college professor at CIA in Denton. Two of the girls became Home Demonstration Agents, Sadie in Texas and Francis in Arkansas.

My dad, John Walthall Oliver Sr., attended Belton High School and Texas A&M College, near Bryan, Texas. He graduated early in 1918 and became a Second Lieutenant, but the war was over by then, so he missed WWI. He returned to A&M and finished his degree work and remained a Reserve and National Guard Officer until he retired in the 1960s.

Dad inherited one hundred fifty acres from his uncle Gus, who also built a nice home for him on the property as a wedding present when he married Elizabeth Miller Oliver. Elizabeth's father was an M-K-T (Missouri-Kansas-Texas) "Katy" Railroad fireman and engineer. She was born in Rosanky, Texas, before the family moved to Belton. Her family of four girls and three boys attended Belton Schools. Her brother Pat built and managed the Big Inch petroleum pipeline that ran from Texas to New Jersey. My dad later bought 42 acres on the north side of his 150 acres to give him a 192-acre farm.

On their farm of 192 acres, my dad and mother raised four children, three born at home, and the last at Scott and White Hospital in Temple. The oldest was Ann, born in 1923, then John Jr. ("Jack") in 1924, Ben D. in 1927, followed by a younger brother, Michael "Mike" Miller Oliver, in 1942. My dad was a Major in the Army at that time, and because war had been declared, my mother bought a bouquet of flowers and drove herself to Scott & White Hospital to have the baby!

My brother Mike was born on November 24, 1942, raised on the family farm, went to Texas A&M, and served twenty-six years in the Air Force, retiring as a Lt Col Engineering Officer. My brother Ben was a banker in Oklahoma for many years and retired in Jayton, Texas, where he manages his wife's and her sister's seventeen section ranch. My sister Ann passed away several years ago.

The writer, John W. Oliver, Jr.—always known as "Jack" Oliver—was raised on his dad's 192-acre farm after his birth on Sept 21, 1924. It was reported by the family and their Doctor Frazier that "Jack" was born at the foot of a rainbow. Aunts arriving to help in the birth observed that the foot of a giant arch of multi-colored light was sitting square on the house as they heard the cry of the new baby.

Jack attended the Three Forks School from first through seventh grades and then Belton High School in the class of 1941. Jack was the principal appointee by Congressman Bob Poage to West Point in 1941 but was unable to accept the appointment because of a ruptured appendix in the fall of 1940 that nearly resulted in his death.

In fact, Jack had an "out-of-body" experience. As he floated above the hospital room, he heard the doctor tell his dad that he could not possibly live and to begin preparations for a funeral. However, Jack's Aunt Lois had stationed herself by his bed for days while he was in the coma. When he held out his hand to her, he regained consciousness. Because there were no drugs, sulfa, or penicillin to administer to Jack, the doctors had packed his body in ice. Three months later, the mess was finally cleaned out of his body. Jack has always insisted—and still does—that credit goes to his Maker for saving his life for some later experience or need.

Following a lengthy recovery, prior to and after surgery, I returned to high school and finished my courses, graduating in 1942. In June of that same year, my dad took me to A&M and dropped me off at Bissell Hall, Home of "E" Battery Coast Artillery. As a "fish" (freshman), it was near-hell for a full semester. At the end of my second term at A&M, I enlisted in the Infantry's Enlisted Reserve Corps on Thanksgiving day 1942. After Christmas, I took the exams for Aviation Cadet Training in the Army Air Corps.

Apparently my year at A&M had prepared me for the exams, because I made three straight nines, the highest scores possible for pilot, navigator, and bombardier training. Much of the exam's content was practical math and problem solving, and I benefited greatly from my years of experience on the farm.

Prior to attending A&M and my appendix bout, I had managed and operated my dad's 192-acre farm by myself. Dad had been called to active duty in 1936 when I was just twelve years old. He bought me an Allis Chalmers two-row planter tractor complete with implements. Mom and my younger brother helped until 1939 when mom joined dad in his service assignments. Consequently, I was alone when my appendix ruptured in 1940.

From the time I can remember—six or seven years old—it was my job to run the one-half to three-quarter mile one-inch water pipeline on a regular basis. I was to make certain that the master control box near grandmother Oliver's home was turned off—or on—to ensure that the flow of windmill water went to the lowest filled tank and to carefully check the entire water line for leaks. By the time I was eight years old, I was a master plumber, could cut and thread metal pipe, insert unions, couplings and cut-offs, and replace gaskets and parts as needed. By the time I was ten in 1934, my brothers and I had jerry-rigged a shower and faucet on our back porch for baths and cleanups—not recommended in winter! The girls still used the number three tub in the kitchen to bathe.

John Fellrath, of Fellrath Plumbing in Belton, often begged dad to allow me to help him on Saturdays to do plumbing jobs under pier-and-beam homes in Belton. He could send me into tight places under homes to repair a problem or replace a plumbing fixture. He paid me well, but I was also fortunate to be able to use his equipment to cut and thread pipe and design cattle watering systems. Mr. Fellrath was like a second father to me because dad was often gone wherever working for the government or serving as a National Guard Officer or Reserve Officer.

Great Uncle Gus had his own water system for the homes of his sister Eunice Oliver and his unmarried sister and Eunice's children still living at home. This included a water well, windmill water lines, control valves, and two large cypress storage tanks. He provided running water to and from these storage tanks to the kitchen sinks of his home—the old Allen home—and to the home he built for his nephew John Oliver and John's wife Elizabeth. Our house did not have a bathroom with a lavatory until early World War II days, and everyone used an outhouse privy. Both homes also had 500-gallon outside storage tanks to catch rainwater from the roofs, and these tanks were also piped to the kitchen sinks in both houses.

Grandmother Oliver put a bathroom in her brother-in-law Gus' house in 1936 after he died. He also had TP&L provide electricity to both homes that same year. The house used by Uncle Gus and Grandmother Oliver used carbide lighting for illumination for thirty years. A carbide pipe system was installed in WWI days. It was okay for room lighting, but poor for reading. My dad waited for electricity, which came rapidly after Roosevelt and his New Deal. As school kids, we used the pressurized pump-up lamps with mantles to study because they provided excellent lighting.

Every couple of years, my Uncle Amos would have me go to the top of the windmill, grease the windmill head, and put oil in the reservoir. He would also lower me down into the well with a rope and bucket to remove mud and dirt from the water basin at the bottom of the shaft. That well was some forty-feet deep, and it was dark and cold. But as long as I knew that Uncle Amos was there, I never worried—I was a tug of the rope away!

Uncle Amos Oliver was our favorite old bachelor uncle on the Oliver side of the family. His only fault, that I could see, was chewing tobacco. I always thought I wanted to chew tobacco with him, but he cured me of that craving by accident one day. When we went into grandma's house for lunch, he would always take the tobacco from his mouth and throw it into the flower bed. Well, one day I was tagging along behind him just far enough and in exactly the wrong position. That tobacco and its juice caught me square in the eyes! I was momentarily blinded and was hurting terribly. Uncle Amos was extremely apologetic and washed out my eyes until they were okay, but I never wanted to chew tobacco or dip again.

I would be remiss if I didn't mention Uncle Amos' cattle. He had a small herd of registered Shorthorn cattle down on his farm on the Leon River. He kept his bull, Butterball, in a bull pen on grandmother Oliver's place after Uncle Gus died. Butterball was a great bull, but he was growing old. We knew never to get in the pen with him even when we brought our milk cows for him to service each year. It was my job, as I got older, to drive—make that walk!—with Butterball on my Uncle Amos' great quarter-horse, as Butterball visited the herd on the Leon and then returned to winter at grandma's.

I wrote an article about Uncle Amos and his cows, his love for registered Shorthorns, and his friendship with Gene Autry, the great showman and movie star. I'd like to share that story now.

UNCLE AMOS

There was a neat article recently in the Temple Telegram about our nationally-renowned cowboy, Les Hood of Killeen, Texas. Les had many followers, and Jack Oliver of Belton, Texas, reported that while he was an admirer, Uncle Amos was a follower. Uncle Amos was known to attend all of the rodeos he could to see Les Hood ride. He would begin at our own Belton Rodeo; go to the Fort Worth Fat Stock Show, journey to Houston's Stock Show, and even on to Kansas City.

Somewhere along the line, Uncle Amos met and became a friend of Gene Autry, the actor and singing cowboy. Both were avid Shorthorn cattle breeders, and they would check out the Shorthorn stock carefully at the stock shows. One year at Fort Worth, Gene Autry asked Amos if he would consider buying a $10,000 registered Shorthorn bull from Scotland. If they both bought one, it would help reduce shipping costs. Accordingly, Uncle Amos and Gene each bought one of those $10,000 bull calves to be shipped from Scotland, the British Isles.

Well, Uncle Amos Oliver got a crackerjack! He named his prized bull *Butterball,* built him a special pen, and cared for him daily. They became close friends. All the while, Uncle Amos was sorting through his small herd of Shorthorn cows, keeping only the best in the herd. When Butterball became of age, size and interest, Uncle Amos moved him to his cattle farm two miles east on the Leon River. There Butterball made himself at home with the prettiest bunch of Shorthorn cows in the country.

Soon Amos' Butterball and those pretty Shorthorn cows had several good-looking calves. About this time, Hubert Martin of Mason, Texas, whose entire family consisted of old Shorthorn breeders, became Belton High School's Agriculture Teacher.

Hubert asked Amos, "Amos, you've got some top notch show calves. What are you going to do about it?" Amos decided to let any dedicated "Ag" student, Future Farmer, or 4-H Club member have a calf for one hundred dollars if they agreed to feed out the calf and guarantee to show it in a major stock show.

As it turned out, Uncle Amos Oliver assembled some top notch kids who were interested, and the very first year one of them won Grand Champion Steer at the Fort Worth Fat Stock Show. Gene Autry was on hand and was as proud of that calf as Amos Oliver was. Uncle Amos had a rule that if one of his calves won Grand Champion at any of the major shows, the young winner could have the pick of the calves the following year. Well, he soon had winners at Fort Worth and Houston.

But the best was yet to come several years later! It seems that a young girl from a nearby county picked one of Uncle Amos' calves. She not only won Grand Champion Steer at Fort Worth but also went on to win Grand Champion Steer at the American Royal Kansas City Fat Stock Show. You can bet Uncle Amos and Gene Autry were there to congratulate that girl!

Now let's roll forward a couple of years to the Fat Stock Show in Fort Worth. Lots of local folks spoke "tongue-in-cheek" about Amos' friendship with Gene Autry. "Probably just a tall tale," they reasoned. Well let's just see about that!

I was pretty close to my Uncle Amos and I would hear people talking, but I didn't pay much attention to it. But one day, a month or so ahead of the Fort Worth Fat Stock Show, Uncle Amos seemed pretty intent on Jack Oliver going to the stock show with him. He even asked my mom and dad, who of course thought it was a great idea that I go.

We drove up to Fort Worth in Uncle Amos' old clunker. He was not much for show and usually wore old khakis and a shirt with the top button buttoned—but never a tie! He looked pretty much like an old cowpoke. Well, when we got to the show, he reminded me that we were going to the rodeo and I was to meet him at the gate on time. "Remember, *on time,*" I heard him shout after me as I went off to check the rows of beautiful livestock.

Hours later I met Uncle Amos at the entrance to the rodeo—on time—and we went in. An usher asked Uncle Amos if he could help him, to which he replied, "Where is Gene Autry's box seat?" I nearly fell out of my boots, as did the rangy usher. Uncle Amos insisted, and we were escorted to the stands. One of Gene's hands soon met us, and we were accompanied to our seats in Gene's box, just the two of us! It then dawned on me that I had seen advertisements that Gene Autry was to be the leading star introducing the rodeo. About then, Gene Autry stepped onto the stage over the bull loading chutes, gave his hello, and then started singing. After a song or two, he looked around the crowd until his eyes settled on our box!

Gene Autry said, "Folks, I want you to meet an old friend of mine who is sitting in my box—Amos Oliver, a well-known Shorthorn cattle breeder." I'll swear, my Uncle Amos got an ovation! Then Gene said—and I'll remember it to my dying day— "Jack Oliver, stand up! Please welcome Amos Oliver's nephew and companion!"

Needless to say, Amos and Jack Oliver enjoyed the rodeo that day! And of course, the word got out about Amos Oliver being Gene Autry's friend and fellow Shorthorn cattle breeder. And as for old Butterball, he just kept grinding out those wonderful show calves and they continued winning the shows. Amos never changed his price or rules in dealing with the Young Future Farmers and 4-H students until he finally went out of business.

Yep, Uncle Amos Oliver was Gene Autry's friend, and those kids would never have had the opportunity to acquire and to show those calves if Gene and Amos had not decided to go for broke and get those two Shorthorn bull calves from Scotland of the British Isles.

Farming was tough but profitable. Besides making me tougher than a boot and preparing me physically for the ordeal, I was setting money aside for college. I raised corn, oats, hay, and cotton. In my senior year in high school, I had the first bale of cotton in Bell County and received a fifty dollar bonus.

Every penny I made I tucked away in my bank account at the Peoples National Bank. That was college money to go to Texas A&M. I raised Shorthorn calves and Hampshire pigs that I showed at Fort Worth and Houston stock shows. The money I got for them went into the fund. Even when we applied for an appointment to West Point, I continued saving for college. It paid off when I finally enrolled at Texas A&M.

At the end of my first year at A&M, the Army Air Corps notified me of my aviation cadet class, reporting March 1, 1943. I had always wanted to be a pilot and had about twenty hours as a pilot trainee, soloing in an Interstate Aircraft *Cadet* trainer at Coulter Field in Bryan, Texas, on September 10, 1942. But it was not to be! The powers-that-be sent me to the first Bombardier-Navigator Course at Concho Field, San Angelo, Texas. I graduated on October 23, 1943, received my wings and my Second Lieutenant bars, and then proceeded to Salt Lake City to join a B-24 crew as their Bombardier. We trained on a B-24 bomber in

Alamogordo, New Mexico, and Charleston, South Carolina, until February 1, 1944, and then departed for combat in Italy.

The minute we arrived at our San Pancrazio base in Italy, the first week of March 1944, I was pulled off of my crew and flew my first five combat missions as a Navigator for a crew whose navigator was killed the day before! From then on, I flew half of my fifty-three missions as Navigator. The remaining missions were flown with my old crew as Bombardier. Our group commander, T.Q. Graf, who was a friend of our state senator Roy Sanderford of my home town, always wanted me to fly with him when he was lead. This gave him a third head if he lost his Bombardier or Navigator. And this we did.

We lost a lot of people. In the six months I was flying my fifty-three missions, we had one hundred percent turnover (losses)—over fifty airplanes and over five hundred men! I received two Purple Hearts, being hit and wounded twice, once on my 16th mission and again on my 53rd. I was lucky to have survived. So many of my friends were lost to anti-aircraft fire or to enemy fighters! As I said, one hundred percent turnover and losses in just six months! Our Group lost 169 airplanes and 1,479 men in two years.

Yes, the members of my bomb group were my family, and the losses cut deeply. I am the only survivor of my ten-man crew. My wife and I are active in my 376th Heavy Bomb Group Veterans Association reunion activities every year. There were eighty Yugoslavian Airmen with their four B-24 bombers who flew with us. We wear their wings. All of them are gone, as are most of our old-timers. Our mean age is eighty-seven, and I am a youngster at eighty-six. A couple at ninety-one and ninety-two still attend. We have over five hundred members in our 376th

Veterans Association. Most are life members but unable to make the reunions. Last year 150 attended in Washington, DC, and visited the WWII Memorial. A total of fifty-one of our WWII fliers attended and around fifty wives and fifty of our children.

Upon my return from combat, I volunteered for Pilot Training, finally graduated, and became a pilot in February 1948. In November 1947, I had received a Regular Army Commission and shortly thereafter elected to make the Air Force a career.

But now back to our B-24 crew, training, and overseas tour in Italy and over Europe/Balkans.

Our B-24 crew formed up at the Alamogordo, New Mexico, Army Air Field in late November 1943. The pilot, co-pilot, navigator, and bombardier came down from Salt Lake City. The remainder of the crew, the engineer, radio operator, tail and ball turret operators, and waist gunners all reported in just ahead of their arrival. All the crewmen spent several days getting checked out in an old B-24D. After a couple of weeks, the Army Air Corps decided to move the entire training group and all of its assigned personnel to the east coast at Charleston Air Field, South Carolina—often appropriately called Ten-Mile Station because it was situated ten miles north of the city of Charleston. The majority of the flight crews and cadre of personnel traveled by troop train from Alamogordo to Charleston, South Carolina.

My dad had given me his old '36 Ford two-door and I requested to drive it through. The vice-commander approved when I agreed to leave it with the training cadre when we departed for overseas. Young and innocent, I figured I could pick it up upon my return from wherever we went. I drove into Charleston early in December 1943, joined my crew, and started training as their Bombardier. I had both ratings—Bombardier and Navigator—but had volunteered to join any crew as bombardier in order to get an earlier crew assignment and deployment overseas.

Christmas and the New Year were rapidly approaching, so we were trying to complete our training requirements early in order to deploy to Cuba shortly into the New Year. Right after Christmas day, my dad called from Fort Meade, Maryland—where he was a headquarters commandant—and stated that he and my mom were taking the east coast train down to Charleston to celebrate New Year's Day with me before I deployed overseas. My pilot, R.L. Johnson, and the training director approved a couple of days off for me, so I started looking for a place for us to stay. The famed Francis Marion Hotel was sold out, as was every other place in town. Our tail gunner had found a mini-motel on one of his exploits and suggested it to me, which I quickly grabbed. To say that it was marginal would be an understatement—and there was no place to eat!

The three of us—dad, mom and I—plus some of my crew, enjoyed New Year's at the base club. The next morning we got up, dressed, and took off to find a place to eat—but nothing was open. The dining room at the Francis Marion was closed. But, lo and behold, there was a small delicatessen next door just opening! The three of us went in to get something to eat—anything! No problem! It was well-stocked (and even more so for a fresh young Second Lieutenant). There were two of the cutest young girls there to wait on us!

I looked them up and down and told my mom I was going to get a date with one of them. My mom pointed out the one she liked, but I really liked the other one—she was as cute as a bug's ear. I told mom, "That is the one!" Mom said, "No, I like the other one." I dropped the argument, and we picked out something to eat. As we were leaving, the girl I had chosen—Miriam—waited on us as mom visited with the other one. This gave me a chance to ask her for a date. Well, it was a big "NO!" right off and she added, "I don't go out with any fly-boys!" Dad saw what was going on, so he took mom outside to the car. Meanwhile, I persisted! Finally, she agreed that I could come calling, but only if her big sister and husband were present.

Mind you, this was on January 1, 1944, in Charleston, South Carolina. Two days later, I went calling. Miriam's sister and her husband had to leave, but we were left in the safe-keeping of her nephew. She fixed me some hot chocolate and we did some light visiting, but it was from across the room. It was pretty cool there at first, but she finally agreed that I could call again two nights later. Her folks came in, and I gave them a rundown on me, my family, and where I came from. Her brother-in-law and sister liked the fact that my dad was an old Army colonel from a farm in Texas. I dressed up and called on her two days later.

This time she agreed to go for a ride with me when she found out that that old '36 Ford was mine—she had thought it belonged to my folks. We drove down and around the Battery overlooking the Charleston harbor. Those old '36 Fords had bucket seats, so she was safe and far away. It was that way for several evenings, but she used the time to get to know everything about me, from birth, life on the farm, high school, and my year in college before enlisting—and who and where my girlfriends were. At the end of the week as I was softly telling her goodnight, she let me kiss her. I was "in love"! We courted for another week before I asked her to marry me. That stunned her, but the next day I brought it up again. She said I would have to ask her mother. Now, her mother was Southern Baptist and lived up-country.

It had been sixteen days since I had met Miriam, and we spent a Sunday with my four gunners who all wanted to meet her. We picnicked on the Citadel Military College grounds. The guys approved—they were my family. The following Saturday, the three crew officers took us to the club for dinner. They quietly approved but said I was crazy. On the 21st day of our courtship, my Miriam's big sister took us up to her dad and mom's to ask permission. It was a cool night, but even a colder reception! Miriam's mom was not happy and told us so. Her dad took me to the kitchen, got out his flask, and we had a shot. We hit it right off. He then left me in the kitchen and went to see his wife. In a little bit, he came back for me and told me to ask her now. I did, and she reluctantly agreed, but only if we got married in the church.

The next week we rounded up a Baptist preacher and he insisted on our being married in his parsonage. Miriam's mother agreed, so we went down to city hall to get our marriage license, where we found out our full names and real ages. Yes, I was nineteen years old and she was a year younger, so all was legal. We were married on January 30, 1944, thirty days after I met her on January 1, 1944, in that neat little delicatessen in Charleston, South Carolina. Our crew stood by us; and our tail-gunner, Wally Trust, loaned me the money for the rings. Wally ended up with five ME-109 kills, and his picture is in the 376th Veterans Association history book. We honeymooned at the Francis Marion hotel for a couple of days and then found a rental two blocks away. A few days later, my crew and I left for Cuba for a week's deployment and remote training.

After we returned from deployment, Miriam and I continued our honeymoon for a long weekend. Then the crew—all ten of us—packed our duffle-bags, told our loved ones goodbye, and left for Mitchel Field, Long Island, New York, to pick up our new B-24J, nose turret and all. The pilot told us on the second day that we would be there five days, and—except for the engineer, his assistant and radio operator—we could take off for New York City for three days. I called Miriam, and she came up the next day. We stayed at the Waldorf Astoria Hotel for the three days. Now that was a honeymoon, with all the New York show and trimmings!

Five days after we arrived at Mitchel Field, we loaded ourselves into that old B-24J and headed south through the Caribbean to Belem on the Brazilian Amazon, then across to Dakar, up to Bengasi, and on to our base at San Pancrazio, Italy. In Italy, I flew my fifty-three missions, about half with my crew and the remainder as Navigator with other crews. We lost so many friends and other crew members—nearly a one-hundred percent turnover in six months! And even though I was hit twice and awarded two Purple Hearts, I never doubted I would return home to my Miriam. I had promised to fly a few more missions for a friend sent to Bari for a month; but after I was hit on my 53rd mission, my squadron commander offered me an opportunity to go home. I accepted and soon left for Naples, where I caught a navy ship on its maiden voyage to Norfolk, Virginia—nearly home.

Miriam had a job as the cashier for the Francis Marion Hotel in Charleston while I was overseas. When I called her from Norfolk, Virginia, she left the next day by train to meet me at Fort Meade, Maryland. Dad had orders for overseas and England, so he gave us his car to drive to Texas. My mother and kid brother road the train home. Miriam and I continued our honeymoon, going to California for R&R (rest and recuperation) following my overseas combat. I taught Navigation at several bases and then went to Army Pilot Training in 1947 and received a regular Army commission. Miriam was my wife and partner, sweetheart and lover, for thirty years in the military. We had three children, one of which is our current 376th Veterans Association Chaplain. We were married sixty-seven years on January 30, 2011.

Jack and Miriam Oliver, 513th Squadron, 376th Heavy Bomb Group, are active to this day in the 376th Heavy Bomb Group Veterans Association. Jack and Miriam returned to Italy several years ago and toured from Milan to Venice, to the Leaning Tower of Pisa, to the Isle of Capri south of Naples, and to the old base location, near San Pancrazio, Italy. The whole town turned out. Jack was selected to give the visitors' speech to the town Mayor and its citizens. The landing strip was still there from which we flew our fifty odd missions. We hugged and cried and remembered our many crew members who were lost—over sixteen hundred men in the two years they were in Italy, and five hundred men and fifty planes in my six-month period in 1944. Our bomb group was one of a half-dozen that flew the August 1, 1943, low-level mission from Benghazi, Tripoli, to the Ploesti oil fields, losing half of the crew on the attack. Our B-24 crew returned to the States in the fall of 1944, but it was July of '45 before the group came home. The European war was over! Now to end the war with Japan in 1945....

Dropping the two atomic bombs from B-29s, on first Hiroshima on August 6, 1945, and then Nagasaki, on August

9, 1945, rapidly brought the war to an end on August 14th. The peace treaty was signed on the deck of the battleship Missouri in Tokyo Harbor on September 2, 1945.

My brother Ben was in the Pacific, a Navy Helmsman on a sea-going tug. He elected to come home. I was teaching Navigation at the San Marcos Airport, Texas, awaiting my Army Pilot Training Class. I chose to stay in the military. My dad was in a military hospital in McKinney, Texas, and later at Brooks General in San Antonio, recovering from WWII wounds. It was more than two years before he was released to come home in 1948. My mother returned home in 1944 from Fort Meade, Maryland, because dad went to the battle of Europe, out of England. She ran his 192-acre farm for him, with some neighbors' help, until his health improved and he was able to come home. He continued to run his farm until his WWII wounds finally put him back into the VA hospital in Temple, Texas, for several years, until his death in 1990.

If it had not been for my dad's far-reaching look into the future, I would not have returned to Texas in 1972, or for many years, if ever. In 1952–53 dad asked me to buy into a 208-acre farm he thought we should purchase through the Texas Veterans Land Board. I finally agreed, and in a few years he sold his interest in the farm to me. It proved to be a solid investment and a great place to get away from the pressure of my military jobs. It also tied me to the land—my land. When we retired from the Air Force after thirty years, we came home to our 208-acre farm, built a new home, and lived on the place for twenty-five years. It was home. But when we did come home in 1972, dad then sold us forty acres of his own 192-acre farm, where we all were born and raised. Could it be that he had been planning for us to truly come home?

Jack and Miriam Oliver

②

SCHOOLING

My schooling started in my Cradle Roll class at three–four years of age in an old Methodist country church in the Three Forks Community east of Belton, Texas. I remember one episode in which our teacher, Mrs. Lucille Dice, assembled us outside on the grass in our Cradle Roll chairs. Class was progressing nicely—I was upside down on the chair with my head on the ground. When my mother came by, she jerked me up by my feet, telling me to sit and pay attention. Mrs. Dice said, "Elizabeth, I don't care which way he is pointing as long as he pays attention!" We loved Mrs. Lucille and we paid attention. It didn't make any difference which way we were pointing.

My mother believed in educating her kids, so we all started early. A friend of hers organized a Kindergarten school in Belton, so off we went at four and five years of age to learn our numbers, ABCs, and how to get along with other kids.

At six years of age, we were enrolled in the first grade at the Three Forks two-room school house. Our teacher was Mrs. Isla Chafin and I was in love. I have always loved my teachers. They became very special. But I got my first and only whipping from Mrs. Isla. One day, she spanked my best friend, John Raymond Henderson, for some prank. When I took his side and threw my best agate marble at her, she promptly snatched me up and I received my deserved spanking. I was sent to the cloak room to think over the error of my ways.

Mrs. Isla had us for four years, and then we moved to the other room for our 5th, 6th, and 7th grades under Mrs. Gladys Cline. I was in love yet again. Mrs. Cline could—and did!—tell the best stories. She could read anything, especially History and Geography, and you'd think you were there. She was the only person I ever knew who could make math interesting. On top of that, she could sing.

She organized a glee club and they could also sing. That's when I found out I couldn't carry a tune in a bucket. But never fear, she made me her assistant, to care for all the music, hand it out, and do the chores. I loved it and never knew I couldn't sing!

When it was time to go to high school, they divided our school district. The east half of Three Forks attended Little River Academy and the west side went to Belton High School, eighth through the eleventh grades. There were only eleven grades through WWII.

We went to Belton High School. I started the eighth grade in the fall of 1937. We were assigned to the first school bus owned by Belton High. It was called the *Cracker Box* because it was wood and looked like a box. Mr. Warsham was our driver, and we minded or our folks would hear about it—and that was not good in those days!

My first day of high school was certainly eventful. I met two senior football players right off on the steps of the high school—Robert Moss and Jamie Wilson. I was not a large or tall person, and as I came up the steps Robert told Jamie, "This one's too small for high school!" So one grabbed me by the feet, the other by my arms, counting, "One, two, three," and tossed me off the high school porch into the bushes. I came out of the bushes mad as a wet hen, but they were gone and I was already late to my first class. My teacher, Mrs. Mildred Pittman, was not upset because she had heard them talking and was very nice to me. I was in love with my teacher again. She ended up with my deepest respect, and she was my history teacher all through high school. She made Texas History, along with Sam Houston, Bowie, and other heroes come alive. American History was the same with George Washington, Daniel Boone, and others. Then, world, old-world, and ancient history, plus the bible—she could tie it all together.

I always wanted to be a Texas Aggie, go to Texas A&M, be an Ag teacher in high school or a county agent. Being born and raised on a farm and running a 192-acre farm for all my high school years certainly prepared me. My dad graduated from A&M in 1918 and was commissioned in the Army. After the end of WWI he returned to A&M for more education. In the 1920s he became an officer in the Texas National Guard and rose to command Company I, 143rd Infantry Texas National Guard in Belton, Texas. In 1935 he was promoted to Captain and left the Guard to become Commander of the CCC (Civilian Conservation Corps) Camp at Mother Neff State Park south of McGregor, Texas. In 1937, dad was transferred to the Colorado River Inks Dam site. He could no longer keep one eye on his farm. He turned to me and asked if I could do it if he got a new AC (Allis Chalmers) two-row tractor. I was a new freshman in Belton High School and thirteen years of age! Dad helped put the crops to bed for the year and turned the reigns of managing and operating the farm over to me. Little did the Belton High Ag Teacher, Hubert Martin, know what he had in store for himself. Hubert Martin was an Aggie and one of the finest men I have ever known. I took three years of agricultural studies under him in high school and worked with him in my senior year as President of the FFA (Future Farmers of America), assisting on all projects. I fed out Hampshire pigs and Shorthorn calves, made every show I could, but preferred the Houston and Fort Worth Fat Stock Shows. When I sold an animal, I banked the money at the Peoples National Bank in my Texas A&M fund. I used my farm crop income for the farm.

A&M nearly lost me at the end of my junior year in high school. I was cutting hay with the tractor and cycle mower when I came down with a terrible stomach ache. I kept working, but it got worse. Finally after nearly collapsing, I was able to guide the tractor to my grandmother's. My Aunt Lois took me to the doctor and to Scott & White Hospital. I had a ruptured appendix and was deathly sick. When I was near death, I received a great honor—the Principal Appointee to West Point for 1941. I was also honored by an out-of-body experience associated with the coma I was in. I knew no one for ten days. I found myself—in my mind—floating in the air over my hospital room and a hallway. The doctor was telling my dad I could not live. I looked down at my Aunt Lois who was sitting by my bed, and I was gone. She held her hands up praying, and I reached down to her hands. She clasped my hand, and I woke up from the coma—in bed this time—with her holding my hand. Yes, there is a God. But what purpose does he have for me? I had been packed in ice for two weeks. There was no medication because there were no penicillin and sulfa drugs to spare at that time. They could not cut me open and allow gangrene to take over, so I was not operated on for ninety days to let the mess in my stomach coagulate. The operations involving clean-out and snipping of adhesions were successful, but too late for the West Point Appointment. I was not unhappy. I was still alive, and I still had my savings for Texas A&M.

I nearly ended up being the next Oliver *ghost*, but my aunt Lois took my hand! Her sister Francis—my aunt—often told me of the three ghosts of our old family homestead, where her uncle Ben had married the widow Allen and moved into her home. Our three ghosts were quite real to several family members, including our son John who reported seeing the same three ghosts without ever knowing they had been observed earlier. John reported a man known by the family as uncle "George" Curb; a little girl—a Houseright child—who had been scalded to death and skipped through the house in a white pinafore dress; and a young Black boy, who lived in uncle Ben's tack room but met an untimely death and was buried on the property. The Oliver children and their friends often put toys and sea shells on the little Houseright girl's grave. I often spent the night with my aunt Lois and uncle Amos, but I never was privileged to see the ghosts. I am responsible for the Allen-Oliver Cemetery and can assure you I look after the little Houseright girl's grave, sea shells, and other gifts to her.

Uncle George Curb—one of our three ghosts—was remembered as a brother to Louis Curb of Killeen, Texas. It was reported that the Curbs and Olivers came to Texas after the Civil War and that they came to visit our uncles Ben and Gus on an annual basis in the late 1890s and early 1900s. Some older Olivers say that *George* might have been a nickname for their lifelong friend.

Our Congressman Bob Poage never started anything he didn't finish, so the next spring he gave me the Principal Appointment to the Naval Academy. All went well, but I flunked the Medical Exam. One had to have a height of five feet six inches at that time to go to the Naval Academy, and I was five feet four inches tall. So back to my original plans to go to Texas A&M! I had lost one semester of High School with the appendix problem, so I was delayed while I made up several courses. Therefore, instead of graduating from high school with my class of 1941, I walked across the stage with the class of 1942 in May and promptly departed for summer school at Texas A&M in June.

My first semester at A&M was taken during the summer and the second semester in the fall on-campus. I was in the Corps of Cadets, assigned to "E" Battery Coast Artillery in Bissell Hall adjacent to the parade ground. Our sophomores whipped us freshmen into shape pretty fast. It was "No Sir," "Yes Sir," and "Which Way Sir?" twenty-four hours a day. I never ran into anything that could touch the Aggie discipline—and those sophomores—in all of my years in the service.

World War II was on, and after Pearl Harbor on December 7, 1941, everyone wanted to get into the fight and go into combat. I was no exception. Our Commandant, Colonel Welty, had a Sergeant Major who had worked with my dad at Fort Sam Houston. SGM Dunbar asked me one day if I wanted to take the exams in Houston to go to Aviation Cadets. I reminded him that one had to be a sophomore. He disregarded my concern and said he had a bus going to Houston the next day for applicants to take the exams. If I passed, he would get me sworn into the Army's Enlisted Reserve Corps, and I could then transfer to the Air Corps for Aviation Cadets. Needless to say, I was motivated and passed the cadet exams and the flight physical. SGM Dunbar was elated. Because it was Thanksgiving weekend, he prepared the paperwork so that my dad could swear me in on Thanksgiving Day. Dad came home for the holiday from the Army at Fort Sam Houston where he served as a Major and Commander of the "Recallee" Center at Fort Dodd. Dad swore me into the Army's Infantry Reserve; but a few days later, SGM Dunbar had me transferred to the Army Air Corps. I was assigned to an Aviation Cadet Class, reporting on-or-about March 1, 1943, for Bombardier training at Concho Field, San Angelo, Texas. We were to be the first class of "Bombagators" (Class 43-13DR) graduating October 23, 1943. We were trained as both Bombardiers and Navigators.

Upon graduation, I was commissioned a Second Lieutenant (2LT), presented my Wings on October 23, 1943, and given orders to go to Salt Lake City to meet the other three officers on our B-24 ten-man bomber crew—the pilot, co-pilot and naviga-tor. I was assigned as Bombardier, although I was newly dual-rated. Two weeks later, the four of us went to Alamogordo, New Mexico, to meet our remaining six crewmen and get acquainted with the B-24 bomber. We met our engineer, radio operator, tail and ball turret operators, and the two waist gunners. We flew and flew that ol' B-24 and got to know each other extremely well.

After only two or three weeks at Alamogordo—where we were getting acquainted with each other, our duties, and that old B-24—orders came down transferring the Bomb Group (100th) and all members and trainees to Charleston Army Air Field, Charleston, South Carolina—with no delays or leaves en route. Most of the men were loaded on troop trains and the permanent cadre flew the airplanes, all to Charleston. Crew training immedi-ately commenced again without a day off. By Christmas, we were pretty well acquainted with the B-24 and tactical and bombing maneuvers.

No time off was given for Christmas or the holidays! Flying and training continued at a fast clip. However, my dad—now an Army Lieutenant Colonel (LTC) and headquarters Commandant at Fort Meade, Maryland—called and asked if he and my mother could come down by train for New Years. Permission was granted, but there were no guest quarters on the base for dependents; nor was there a hotel room in Charleston to be found. Our tail gunner had located a small motel a couple of miles out on the Columbia, South Carolina, highway. We grabbed it. It wasn't much, but at least we were together. We celebrated the New Year, 1944, at the officers club and slept at the motel.

New Year's Day January 1, 1944, found us with no place to eat. Everything was closed, including the restaurant at the Francis Marion Hotel downtown. This we found out after driving the ten miles into town. But there was a delicatessen that was open next door to the hotel and with food to buy. We hit it hard, buying orange juice and all the breakfast trimmings we needed. Remember, this was January 1, 1944, and on this date, in this store, I met the girl who was to be my bride thirty days later on January 30, 1944! When I met her there and told my mother, she nearly died. Yes, we were married after a fast courtship between B-24 flights, and I left for overseas a few days later. Mom said it wouldn't last, but we celebrated our 67th Anniversary on January 30, 2011. When you see a jewel, you go after it, whatever the cost, time or situation!

Combat called. We departed to Cuba for overseas and over-water training in the middle of February 1944. We came back through Charleston in late February to recover our gear and went to Long Island's McGuire Field to pick up a new B-24J for our trip to Europe—via the southern route: Puerto Rico, Trinidad, Belem/

Natal on the Amazon River, across to Dakar in Africa, then on to Marrakech in Morocco, and to Tunis, North Africa. No delay, that same day, it was on to San Pancrazio, Italy!

Schooling and training—and more of it—followed by even more schooling and training! I was served well by my background on the farm, our community church, the Three Forks School, Belton High School, and Texas A&M, all of which never for a minute let up on the training and instruction. I was to need every minute of every training moment to survive fifty-three combat missions. That went for everyone on our crew. It was a close-knit team that worked together to accomplish our combat missions and to survive for another day.

I was hit by flak on my 16th mission and again by twenty millimeter cannon fire on my 53rd mission, earning two Purple Hearts. I also was awarded the Distinguished Flying Cross (DFC), Air Medal with five Oak Leaf Clusters, and two Group Commendation Medals for some highly successful combat missions. Six of our ten crew members were hit by enemy flak or fighter aircraft fire. All survived fifty missions, and all came home in the fall of 1944. However, I am the only survivor of the crew of ten, having recently lost our pilot, R.L. Johnson, and our engineer, SGT Roterd, in 2010 and 2009 respectively.

Since I couldn't return to Texas A&M for that degree, as the war was still on, and I'd also wanted to be a pilot since childhood, I asked to go to Army Air Corps Pilot Training. This request was approved, and after much waiting and the closing of many Army Air Corps bases, several hundred of us finally reported to pilot training at Randolph Field near San Antonio, Texas, in early February 1947.

Pilot training was tough, and they made it even tougher. The Army didn't need aviators in 1947, and an aspiring pilot was *washed out* (eliminated) for any insignificant reason. All student officers, most having been in WWII, took it seriously. We wanted to be pilots and to make the new Air Force a career. We also had the first class of aviation cadets to go through with us, the first since WWII.

We were the last class to fly the *Stearman*, the bi-wing primary trainer, and the first to fly the T-6 *Texan* trainer in Basic. Our class was split after basic training. Half went to multi-engine aircraft at Barksdale, Louisiana, in B-25s (twin-engine) and B-17s (four-engine). The remaining students went to Williams AFB, Arizona, to fly single-engine fighters. We flew the famous WWII fighter, the P-51 *Mustang*, through advanced training. It was fantastic! Ten of us were also selected to fly the new P-80 *Shooting Star* jet fighter in the last weeks of Advanced. I car-pooled with Joe McConnell—leading jet ace in Korea—and Cecil Foster, who achieved ten jet kills. Bill Shadel and I were tendered Regular Army Commissions while flying the P-80.

A career for me in fighters was apparently not to be. The 1st Fighter Wing at March AFB and its four squadrons scattered around the United States were disbanded. We administrative types—I was the Wing's administrative officer (adjutant)—were all assigned to Kansas City, Kansas, as cadre, to set up the new Central Air Defense Headquarters.

As we got to work, I was assigned to General Frank Robinson as his Secretary to their first Command Promotion Board. General Robinson was an old soldier who maintained that even an ambitious WWII fighter pilot would not go to Korea until every pilot that didn't fight in WWII did so. Because I wanted to go to Korea as a fighter pilot, I repeatedly pressed the General. Eventually, he got tired of my persistence and instead sent me to Panama to fly the C-47 *Gooney Bird*.

We had just become the *United States Air Force* in 1948, but we were still wearing the Army uniform in 1952 and operating under the Army's MOS (Military Occupational Specialty). The new Air Force had USAF personnel in every country in Central and South America as well as Air Attachés with the US Embassies. General Robinson wanted me to go to Panama, visit every country, and convert every Air Force individual's MOS to an AFSC (Air Force Specialty Code). I was also tasked with making certain they were appropriately current in Spanish or Portuguese language skills.

I was trained at Lowry Field in Denver, Colorado, in Personnel Management/Classification and Personnel Assignment and then sent off to Panama on May 17, 1952. Upon my arrival, I was given an old twin-engine DC-3 (C-47) Gooney Bird; a single-engine qualified co-pilot, who had never even been in a C-47; and a new *buck sergeant* engineer, just out of mechanic engineers training. We launched from Mexico City in June of 1952 and covered every country in Central America and every type of airfield. I was getting to know the DC-3; and it was getting to know me, as was my trusty crew—they learned fast!

We were supposed to be converting all those "new" Air Force personnel from Army ways, but everyone expected us to haul their freight and supplies between countries and also to Panama. We became proficient in flying into and out of everywhere and any place and under any conditions. Some dirt fields were rather primitive to say the least. In three months we had covered all the countries of Central America, and by the fall of 1952, we were ready to take on all of the South American countries.

On my 28th birthday, we headed to South America. By then, I wouldn't have traded anything for my crew. They now knew that ol' Gooney Bird! We covered South America country by country. We visited every Air Force Mission and Air Attaché, converting old MOSs to AFSCs and learned a mountain of things about each country, as well as flying peculiarities in and between every country. We were back in Panama for Thanksgiving and began wondering what we would do next.

I had been assigned to the Base Personnel and Administrative Office while I visited all of the Central and South American countries for six months. An old friend, who was the Base Adjutant at Albrook Field in the Canal Zone, became desperately ill and was air-evacuated to a hospital in Washington, DC. I was assigned his job in his absence, but his health precluded his return. I was subsequently permanently assigned as Base Adjutant and Base Personnel Officer, a position I maintained until I rotated back to the States in July 1955.

While I was Base Adjutant, I continued to fly the C-47 throughout Central and South America. I also flew the B-26, towing targets for the Army's anti-aircraft units at Colon, Panama, on the Atlantic Ocean side. I also kept four T-33 jet trainers—being assigned to Venezuela—in flyable storage because of my P-80 jet training experience. I became a T-33 instructor in 1953 and continued as a *T-bird* Instrument Instructor until retiring in 1972.

The University of Maryland had a detachment at Albrook Field, and many of us worked on our degrees, taking the University's courses. In late 1954, I had completed over one hundred hours, and Texas A&M sent me my Aggie senior ring after I sent them $250.

In July 1955, I was reassigned to LSU (Louisiana State University) to teach ROTC (Reserve Officer Training Corps)

Cadets. Our Commander and Commandant insisted that all of his officers work on their degrees or acquire an additional one. AFIT (Air Force Institute of Technology), at the Air Force Air University, insisted I choose a minor. Since I had been a Celestial Navigator before I was a pilot, I chose to take Astronomy. I continued to fly the T-33s and two L-17 Navions while teaching ROTC. I graduated in 1959 from LSU and was sent to Keesler AFB, Mississippi, to brush up on electronics and my math. I continued to instruct in the T-33s. In 1960, I was assigned to Vandenberg, AFB, California, to the Satellite Tracking Station, up on the hill, east of Vandenberg. The various satellite and missile launch pads were down on Vandenberg near the Pacific Ocean, line-of-sight from our tracking station. I was assigned with contractor technicians of Philco-Ford to train as a Satellite Master Controller. The Master Controller tracked satellites in orbit, gave commands, and interpreted data. He also worked with satellites on the launch pads, preparing their communications, electronics, and telemetry for launch.

We had a newly-developed satellite space vehicle called the *Agena* produced by Clarence "Kelly" Johnson's Skunk Works at LMSC (Lockheed Missile and Space Company). The program was known as *Discoverer* research satellite program by the public and *Corona* intelligence imaging platforms by the CIA. The Agena was launched atop a Thor ballistic missile and placed into a polar orbit. The Agena had triple-axis control and cameras whose film was loaded in an ablative nose cone and returned to earth using a parachute. C-119s, and later C-130s, would catch the parachute with cable and hook mechanisms, reel it in, and return the capsule and film to Washington by aircraft. We had various and sundry failures through the 12th Agena launch, but finally a successful launch and recovery. On the 14th flight, we filmed 1,600,000 miles of Russia and returned the film to the CIA in Washington, DC.

Needless to say, the United States had little to no intelligence on the Russian launch complexes or any long range missiles possibly aimed at the United States. President Eisenhower had tried every recognizance means conceivable, from human spies, to a matrix of four hundred balloons overflying Russia, to the U-2 aircraft flown by pilots such as Francis Gary Powers. He wanted the Top-Secret Corona program to be effective and supported us in our failures to ultimately be successful! Once it became a success, the Agena satellite proved itself to be the big workhorse for the United States. The Russians no longer had secretive missiles, ships, submarines, planes, and military complexes.

After completing my training as a Satellite Master Controller, I was trained by LMSC as a Satellite Test Director over the Controllers. I was then given the assignment as Operations Officer over Controllers and Test Directors. I was Operations Officer, twelve-on and twelve-off, for many months of the operational Corona program. At the same time, I was primary for the *MIDAS* (Missile Detection and Surveillance) and back-up for the *SAMOS* (Satellite and Missile Observation System) programs, both highly-classified and restricted to need-to-know.

In January 1962, I was loaned to the AEC (Atomic Energy Commission) to be the JTF-8 (Joint Task Force) FIC (Frequency Interference Coordinator) and JTF-8's Projects Coordinator at the Johnston Island Pacific test site. After getting JTF-8 organized in Washington, DC, under the command of Army General Alfred Starbird and Navy Admiral Steven Mufson, I worked with the AEC in Albuquerque, New Mexico, lining up project facilitators.

I then went to Hawaii as the advance party for JTF-8 to coordinate and facilitate relations between the Air Force, Army, Navy, and their contractors. I was then assigned to the Aircraft Carrier *USS Hornet* which was to be the command post for B-29 nuclear bomb air drops from Christmas Island. Upon completion, I was sent back to Hawaii and to Johnston Island as on-site FIC and Project Coordinator for all Thor-launched atomic/nuclear warheads. Our command post was on the *USNS Range Tracker* missile range instrumentation ship from Fort Magu, anchored in the bay at Johnston Island. At one point, our new launch controller destroyed a warhead a few hundred feet overhead, showering the island with fragments from the nuclear warhead. As FIC, I was asked to identify and label the fragments and then open a path to the chow hall by General Starbird. Even though I cautioned him against being in too big a hurry, due to the scattering of the raw uranium debris, the General insisted.

Of the two hundred or so personnel involved during the incident on Johnston Island that day, I know of only a few who have survived. Our three-star (Lt Gen) project commander of JTF-8, General Starbird, and many others subsequently died of radiation sickness, as did my Army and Air Force Colonel supervisors, COL Ellis Mist and COL Mike Meyer from Johnston Island.

Jack and Miriam Oliver shortly after their wedding in 1944

3

MY SERGEANTS

My dad was commander of the Texas National Guard Company in Belton, Texas, in the early 1930s. He constantly complimented his non-commissioned officers (NCOs), particularly his First Sergeant and Platoon Leaders. As a child, the sergeants made me the mascot for the Company. I found out how important dad's top NCOs really were.

When I went to Texas A&M and joined the Corps of Cadets, the Commandant of Cadets had an old sergeant major, SGM Dunbar, who ran the commandant's office. He was totally supported by Colonel Welty, our Commandant. On my first evening, I was on flag detail. When I turned in the flag after retreat, SGM Dunbar asked that I report to him. When I did, he asked if Lieutenant John Oliver of Belton, Texas, was my dad. He also asked if he had served at Fort Sam Houston. I replied, "Yes, in WWI." He liked and respected dad and offered to help me in any way. Later, at the end of my first year at A&M, SGM Dunbar again called me in to see him. When I reported, he announced that he was sending a bus to Houston for cadets to take the exams for Army Aviation Cadet training. He asked, "Do you want to go?" I told him I wasn't yet a sophomore, to which he countered that I could go anyway. I went, passed all the exams, but was not selected for pilot training. The examiners wanted me to be a Navigator! In spite of my complaints, they gave me a class date in March 1943. I was to train as a Bombardier-Navigator and to remain in school until I received orders. In late February 1943, I received orders to go to the San Antonio's Aviation Cadet Center, register for an Air Force Aviation Cadet class, take a physical, and pass exams to ensure that I could complete the cadet course.

We were all sent to Houston's Ellington Field for pre-flight training to ensure we would be competent, responsible soldiers. After thirty days, we were ordered to our flight school. I was sent to San Angelo, Texas, to enter the Air Corps' first Bombardier-Navigation School. Unfortunately we never got our T-7 Navigation flight trainers, so we graduated on October 23, 1943, as Second Lieutenant Bombardier-Navigators, without our Celestial Navigator wings. Several of us were chosen to go to the San Marcos Celestial Navigation School later, but it was too late for most of the cadets. Most everyone went overseas as Bombardiers on B-24 crews.

I went to Salt Lake City in November 1943 to meet our pilots. We then went to Alamogordo, New Mexico, to meet our crew and get acquainted with the B-24. We met two old Air Force Sergeants, one of whom was to be our flight engineer and the other our radio man. Both were twenty-seven years of age and seasoned tech sergeant NCOs. The other four gunners were all staff sergeants but had been around a bit. We called the crew chief "Pop" and he acted accordingly. Of course, our pilot, Bob Johnson, was the boss, but due respect was given Sergeant "Pop" Roterd, and he had the admiration of all of the crew. Sergeant Roterd remained a friend and advisor until he died in Long Beach, California, in 2009. Our pilot died in

2010 and all others sometime earlier. I am the sole survivor of our ten-man crew.

We didn't pay much attention to rank with our crew. Everyone knew that our pilot ran the show and called the shots on our missions, with Sergeant Roterd being in his ear and on his right shoulder. Without Sergeant Roterd's constant attention to our B-24 and his men, we could not have kept that old B-24 going and finished our missions. That B-24 and Roterd were as one! He knew its soul, every crack and sound.

When I finished my missions and returned to the States in the summer of 1944, I reported in to an old moth-eaten sergeant for reassignment. He noted my two Purple Hearts, ribbons, and new First Lieutenant bars. Then he looked me over and said, "Lieutenant, what can I do for you?" Without hesitation, I ventured, "I want to go to the Army's pilot training, without delay, so I can fly in the Pacific." He said he would certainly sign me up, but he couldn't guarantee a class. To this day, I don't think I would ever have finally been assigned a pilot training class without that old sergeant's help. The Army was cutting all of the cadet schools drastically, and most of the crew members going to the B-29 and other aircraft in the Pacific were already trained and well-qualified. The Army had promised some eight hundred of us war-weary bombardiers, navigators, and engineers that we would have a chance to go to pilot training. And finally, they kept their word and sent us to Randolph Field. After pilot training, there were plenty of flying jobs available because, when the Pacific war closed down, everyone came home and got out of the Air Force. I instructed Reserve and National Guard officers for a year; went to B-29s and flew them for a year; and was then off to March AFB, California, to fly fighters in the 1st Fighter Wing.

I wanted to continue flying full-time as a pilot, especially as a fighter pilot. However, I was a regular Army officer, and I was asked to be the Squadron Commander's Administrative Officer—we called him *Adjutant*. I took the assignment, but was not happy, and flew the P-51 fighter all I could. After a couple of months of working for the Squadron Commander and spending most of my time flying, our First Sergeant—a senior enlisted man who had served in the 82nd Airborne in the Battle of the Bulge—politely asked me if he could visit with me privately. He secured the commander's jeep, and we drove down to the end of the runway to watch takeoffs and landings.

After a bit of chatter, he reminded me that I was a *Regular* Officer and apparently planned to make the Air Force a career. When I agreed, he proceeded to tell me that he didn't think I wanted to make the Air Force a career because I had shown no interest in learning any of the details of running the squadron of two hundred men. Didn't I want to learn about morning reports, squadron reports, military writing, pay records, and payment of the men? I explained that I felt that all that would come in time, and I just wanted to build up my flying time for now. I then suggested that we return to the squadron. I was not happy that this NCO, our First Sergeant, had been so pushy and personal. I left the sergeant and signed out a P-51 to help get the meeting off my chest. Yet, something kept telling me I wasn't acting very smart. I turned in the P-51, didn't fly after all, and looked up Sergeant Johnson! I told him that I was ready to learn. He said he would never be disrespectful, but that I would have to take on the jobs of Morning Report Clerk, Squadron Administrative Clerk, and Squadron Supply Officer if I was to ever learn. I reluctantly agreed. He then gave the existing Morning Report Clerk two weeks off, and I had to do the report. I was awful at it and committed every error possible. In the military, the Morning Report had to be perfect and hand-carried to higher headquarters. After two weeks, I could do the report, no errors. He then gave the Squadron Administrative Clerk two weeks off, and I now received, reviewed, filed, wrote return letters, and asked the Commander for signatures. In most cases, the Commander would have me get with the first sergeant to work things out. I could type, so in two weeks we pretty well had the administration duties down pat. Then two weeks in Squadron Supply! I neither forgot that training nor the respect that I had earned from Sergeant Johnson. He was so proud of me, he bragged to every one of his NCO friends.

In a couple of months, the sergeant major at Group Headquarters had talked his boss, a lieutenant colonel, into taking me as his Adjutant. Now I had *four* squadrons to look after! In two more months, the Base Adjutant and 1st Fighter Wing administrative job came open. The occupant of that position had gone to the hospital for surgery, and I was asked to cover for him until he returned. He never returned, and I remained Wing/Base Adjutant and Top Secret Control Officer until I had to cut the orders disbanding the 1st Fighter Wing. All through those weeks and months, First Sergeant Ed Johnson was always there. Somehow, he would always show up when I needed him. I seldom flew anymore, even the P-51, because I was so busy trying to do the job right. But Sergeant Johnson never let me miss getting my required flying time in. When they dissolved the 1st Fighter Wing, all administrative and non-flying officers went to Kansas City to organize the Central Air Defense Headquarters. Sergeant Johnson went to Spokane, Washington, and stayed there until he retired from the Air Force. After my months with Sergeant Johnson, I never ran into any challenge in personnel or administration at Kansas City—or anywhere else—that I couldn't handle.

Some thirty years later, after I had retired from the Air Force, I had a feeling come to me about Sergeant Johnson. Where was he and why hadn't we heard anything? I knew Sergeant Johnson was a Master Mason, so I called the old Masonic Lodge that he had belonged to in Victorville, California. They told me he was still in Spokane, Washington, and gave me his address and telephone number.

We contacted his wife, who immediately remembered us. She informed us that he was not doing well. We made a plan to be at her door in ten days at a specific time, if she thought it would be all right. She agreed not to tell him and assured us that the surprise was a good idea. Ten days later, we drove up to their home, knocked on the door and Sergeant Johnson answered. Have you ever seen two old fools hugging and crying?—yes, crying! I was just a young foolish Lieutenant when I met Sergeant Johnson, but he saw something in me that, for some reason, I at first had missed. He set me on the right path, in our Air Force, to do nearly impossible things and finally to gain the rank of full Colonel in the highly technical fields of space and missiles. Yes, thank you First Sergeant Ed Johnson, 94th Maintenance Squadron, 1st Fighter Wing, 1948–49!

It seemed like every time I ran into a spot where it would be nice to have someone notice and give assistance, a senior sergeant would always enter the picture on my behalf. It happened in Panama when I was assigned as Base Adjutant/Base Personnel Officer and still expected to fly when my turn came up. Many times, flight assignments would take me away for ten to fifteen days, for example a trip to Rio de Janeiro, Brazil, or Buenos Aires,

Argentina. For some reason or other, I was assigned a senior NCO, a Master Sergeant from a major US Air Force Command. MSgt Baker was the sharpest, neatest, most disciplined person I had ever met. He totally supported me, and I found out that when I had to be gone a few days, he covered my offices and job assignments as if I were there. I never received a complaint from my supervisors, those working for me, or those needing assistance regarding my responsibilities. MSgt Baker had an assistant working for him, MSgt Hungerford, who backed up Sergeant Baker totally. Even when I was on the Good Will Tour around the Americas for many weeks, they covered my jobs—and theirs—without a blemish.

Some years later, I spent several years in the highly classified Space and Missile Programs. The Air Force and the CIA had hand-picked around twenty officers to be trained for, and then man, the Vandenberg AFB Satellite Tracking Station. We assumed our supervisors would grade and rate us accordingly for our efforts, but nothing could be further from the truth. MSgt Hungerford had been assigned to the Pentagon in Washington, DC, and to officer personnel and their files. MSgt Hungerford requested my file, wanting to see what, where, and how I was doing. He was flabbergasted, filed my records, and called me personally. He asked if I had seen my ER (effectiveness report) when it was sent in by my Commander and Operations Officer. Commanders were supposed to review their evaluations of their officers with them before forwarding them on to higher headquarters. They had not! Their reports were typically negative and included downgrading comments. About this same time, I had been the Primary Operations Officer for the key classified *MIDAS* (Missile Detection and Surveillance) satellite program. All went well and I had been commended and awarded the Air Force Commendation Medal for my efforts by General "Red" Moore, our next higher headquarters Commander. Now, another Command Sergeant Major, who worked for General Moore, was reviewing a couple of effectiveness reports for General Moore's endorsement when he took a look at my report. He remembered the General commending me on MIDAS and presenting me with the Air Force Commendation Award. There was obviously no correlation between this downgrading report and the actual performance of the person—in this case, me!

General "Red" Moore went over my effectiveness report with SMSgt James Anderson and instructed Sergeant Anderson to rewrite it for him. The report was to include the commendation on MIDAS and the Air Force Commendation Medal. The sergeant was also told to mark the top ratings and insert the appropriate relative comments for the General to sign. General Moore then called me to Sunnyvale, California, from Vandenberg AFB, showed me both the old and new ratings and subsequently forwarded the revised favorable rating to Systems Command and to the Air Force. After reviewing my reports, and when it seemed the air was clear, I told the General about my previous year's reports and the fact that they had not been reviewed by, or with, any officer at Vandenberg either. I had also checked with our officers, and none had had their rating officers go over their effectiveness reports with them.

Fortunately—at least for me—I was promptly loaned to the AEC (Atomic Energy Commission) for the JTF-8 Pacific atomic tests as a telemetry expert, to be their Frequency Specialist and to be Projects Manager for AEC.

When I returned from temporary duty and the tests, my old commander and his deputy had been reassigned. They could do no more damage at the Vandenberg Tracking Station! Sergeant Anderson was given a reserve commission, went on active duty as an officer, and retired as a full Colonel. But he served us well as a senior sergeant at our satellite headquarters with General Moore.

After serving as Commander of the Satellite Tracking Station in Hawaii for four years and as Chief of Staff of Operations for Space and Missiles in Los Angeles for two years, I went to Fort Monmouth, New Jersey, to be Chief of the East Coast Field Office of the DCA (Defense Communications Agency). It was a great assignment for which I received the Legion of Merit and retired as a full Colonel from the US Air Force.

My retirement required a full physical and recommendation for any disability. Because my wife worked in the hospital and was in charge of the out-patient clinic, she obviously knew the hospital's Command Sergeant Major, CSM King. He volunteered to push my physical evaluation through, but the Joint Command in Washington, DC, turned it down. Sergeant King asked to see me and we went over the reasons for their decision. After some thought, I elected not to fight the issue.

Still, CSM King was not happy and insisted on revising the packet of retirement physical data so that the VA (Veterans Administration) could re-evaluate my records for a recommended disability. He believed strongly that I should have received forty percent disability from my Regular Officer retirement. He received my permission to draw up the packet and send it to the VA's offices in Waco, Texas, for review. Upon my full retirement and settling in near Salado, Texas, I received a notice from the VA in Waco to come in for an evaluation. After several visits, they gave me a fifty percent disability rating. Keep in mind, an old, dedicated sergeant once again came through and greatly helped me! I now have been evaluated at one hundred percent disabled. CSM King retired from the Army and attended law school. He practiced law in Alabama until his death. Just how can I thank so many dedicated and considerate non-commissioned officers for helping me so much before, during, and following those thirty years?

Yes, thirty years! After thirty years of service, my physical abilities deteriorated rapidly. Much of my disability came from an old B-29 aircraft accident in 1949 at MacDill AFB where I broke my back. Considerable effort was made to have my disability accepted by the Air Force as part of the CRSC (Combat-Related Special Compensation) program. The Air Force did not approve my request, but the Veterans Administration felt differently and recommended that I use my further degrading physical condition as leverage to request an evaluation to increase my fifty percent VA disability rating.

The VA was so snowed-under with new evaluation requests that they suggested I go to the Texas Veterans Administration to carry the ball. I did so and was assigned to an old retired Air Force Senior Master Sergeant, Sergeant Retired Dave Samuels. In two weeks, he had completely formulated a request for me to sign to re-evaluate my physical status to upgrade my disability—including doctors' updated evaluations. In less than thirty days, Sergeant Retired Dave Samuels called me to announce that a ninety percent disability was approved. He encouraged me to contest it, which I did. Within a week, the VA approved a one hundred percent disability rating. It is now permanent, and I will continue to receive the disability payment and health care from the Veterans Administration (VA) for the rest of my life.

Our Fort Hood Retiree Council holds an Annual Retiree Day at Fort Hood every fall plus a full weekend of activities to ensure that all retirees are aware of their VA benefits and availability. A retired veteran from Fort Hood and/or the 174-county area of Texas is selected by the Retiree Council to be honored Retiree of the Year. Command Sergeant Major Frank Minosky nominated me to receive this honor and the Council approved. I will be so honored in October 2011 for the ensuing year. There is no greater honor an officer can receive than to be recognized and honored by his sergeants, and of course, the Retiree Council of Fort Hood, Texas.

Lieutenant Jack Oliver

Consolidated B-24 Liberator

(4)

MY GENERALS

I did not have to wait until I entered the military to know about Generals. My father was a close friend of General Walton H. Walker of Belton, Texas. General Walker was General Patton's right hand man as they drove across Europe in WWII. After Germany surrendered, General Walker became Commanding General in Korea. In high school, I did some plumbing work with John R. Fellrath and often ended up on Saturdays at the home of General Walker's mother repairing pipes, stopping leaks, or opening drains. When the General was home, he always visited with me about my dad. Dad had gone to Texas A&M in WWI, and of course General Walker went to West Point. I suppose my interest in West Point came about by talking to General Walker. In 1940, at the end of my senior year in Belton High School, I was principal appointee from our Congressional District for West Point.

I had a ruptured appendix in the fall of 1940 and was not able to accept the appointment to West Point. I nearly died, but upon recovery I entered Texas A&M College, following in the footsteps of my father.

I wanted to fly from the day I was old enough to consider it. I read every article and book about Lindbergh and his wife. I was a fan of Wiley Post and his plane, the *Winnie Mae*, and read of his exploits. I also kept up with General Billy Mitchell and his battle to prove the importance of air power. While I was a freshman at Texas A&M, I took flying lessons and soloed in an Interstate Aircraft *Cadet* trainer at Coulter Field, northeast of Bryan, Texas. General Hap Arnold of the fledging Army Air Forces was my idol, and I read about everything he did.

I was accepted for Aviation Cadets in the Army Air Corps in 1942. I just knew I would be a pilot in WWII. It didn't happen! Instead, I was made a Bombardier and Celestial Navigator.

After flying my fifty-three missions in Europe in 1944 as a Navigator and Bombardier on B-24 Bombers, I applied for pilot training, hoping to make the Air Corps my career. I was assigned as Base Public Relations Officer while waiting for a pilot class. In 1946, I was sent to the Air Corps Public Relations School at the Air University at Selma, Alabama. Our school Commandant was Brig Gen William P. Nuckols. He didn't only command, he taught classes. He was great, having been in media circles in New York City. We learned how to read and write again. We wrote stories and learned how to tell stories as he guided us through the PIO (Public Information Officer) course. He took us to New York City upon graduation to see how the media operated from the top down. We visited Radio City, enjoyed a Rockettes performance, and saw our first television show. We watched Kate Smith and met Edgar R. Murrow. We went to pilot training after we left General Nuckols' school. He left for Korea to chair the peace talks at Pan Mun Jon in Korea.

After entering pilot training at Randolph Field in 1947, we met our next great General—General Cannon. He was over all of the Air Training Command (ATC) activities but was stationed at Chanute Field in Illinois. A Major aide of his was in our pilot training class.

General Cannon came to Randolph on a staff visit and asked to see the Major, who had reportedly washed out of pilot training and was at another air base in San Antonio. General Cannon demanded to see him and found out that the Major had been abused, harassed, and finally dismissed for no cause. All the students knew about the unfair dismissal, and the General found out. He directed that the Major be reinstated, treated as an officer and gentlemen, and be allowed to complete pilot training. The General also relieved the commandant of the pilot school. When we graduated, General Cannon came to our graduation party at the Randolph AFB Officers Club.

In late 1948, I was assigned to Castle AFB at Merced, California, to fly B-29s. The 93rd Bomb Wing Commander/Base Commander was General-elect, Colonel Bob Terrell. In a few years he earned his fourth star and became Commanding General of Air Defense Command (ADC). I had flown as a Navigator on several missions in WWII with Captain Terrell. He could never understand why I was flying B-29s when I was trained to be a fighter pilot and had been jet-fighter qualified in the P-80.

Colonel Bob Terrell's boss was General Curtis Lemay, Commanding General of Strategic Air Command (SAC). He commanded all US long-range bombers and, of course, the B-29 bomb group at Castle AFB, California—Colonel Terrell's outfit. General Lemay was known for dropping in on any of his bases, unannounced.

Apparently, he had let Colonel Terrell know he was coming. I was Airdrome Officer and was expected to greet and care for any transient aircraft and crews. I was told to meet the aircraft, no honors, and be at the beck-and-call of General Lemay.

I met the plane that turned out to be a twin-engine DC-3 Gooney Bird, which the General was flying. The General's engineer made up the entire rest of his crew. General Lemay looked me up and down and asked if I knew the Officers Club's Mess Steward. When I told him that I did, he asked me to take him to see him. Apparently, he had been the General's steward on his airplane. I explained to him that the sergeant was in the kitchen store room, and that I would get him. General Lemay exclaimed, "No, I will go to him!" I did not know at the time that the sergeant was dying. General Lemay pushed by me and stated, "Come back for me in an hour, and I don't want to be bothered!" As I left, I heard the General say, "Give me that flask. Is it good whiskey?" I couldn't help it. I had to stop and watch the General toss one to his old side-kick.

I picked the General up promptly one hour later and took him to his Gooney Bird. He hugged the old sergeant as we left and told him "Goodbye." Throughout my career, all I had ever heard about General Lemay was that he was a hard-ass SOB. I will never believe it. All I saw was the kindest and most gentle Commanding General I'd ever seen.

The sergeant died in less than a month. You can bet I went to his funeral. Colonel Terrell never mentioned the visit, except to say, "Take care of that Sergeant!"

SAC had one fighter outfit at March AFB near Riverside, California. After about a year, Colonel Terrell called me in one Friday morning and asked if I still wanted to fly fighters. Well, he informed me that if I kept quiet and reported to a friend of his the following Monday at the 1st Fighter Wing, I could have my wish.

I went, and his staff handled my family's departure right behind me. I got to fly the P-80 and P-51 fighters while I waited for an opening to fly the new F-86 fighter plane. *General* Terrell followed my career until he died. The 1st Fighter Wing closed down before I ever got to fly the new F-86, but I was able to enjoy many an hour in the P-51 Mustang.

I was assigned to and helped organize the new Central Air Defense Force in Kansas City, Missouri, in February 1951. I was the Headquarters' Squadron Adjutant and flew DC-3 Gooney Birds and the C-45 *Twin-Beech*. Enter my next general, Brig Gen Frank Robinson. He was to chair the Command's first Promotion Board. The General knew my squadron commander, and he picked me to be the Board's Secretary. I ran everything for him and learned to love and respect him. After my Board duties were completed, he put me in charge of Officer Personnel in Headquarters. The Korean War was in full swing, and I wanted to go as a fighter pilot, putting my name on every list to go to Korea. He would raise hell, take my name off of the list, and tell me emphatically that I couldn't go "until the last SOB that didn't go over in WWII went!" After a couple of months, he called me in and told me he had my overseas assignment. I asked what I would be flying in Korea, and he thundered back, "You're not going to Korea, you're going to Panama. You're going to fly DC-3s, the *Gooney Birds!*" He reminded me that we were a new Air Force, and I was being sent to Panama to convert everyone's MOS (Military Occupational Specialty) designation to the new AFSC (Air Force Specialty Code). As he dismissed me, he said, "I'll be needing you when you come home. Keep in touch and bring me a six pack of old Matus rum anytime you come to the States." I never got to serve with him again, but I guarantee you that I brought him a six pack of rum every time I came to the States on a trip! General Robinson put me in a position to fully learn all of the facets of personnel and administration in the Air Force and made me a thorough and safe Gooney Bird pilot. I only lost one engine in three full years of flying in South and Central America.

While I was assigned at Albrook Field, Panama, as Personnel Officer and Base Adjutant, I was asked to be Major—later Brigadier General—Chuck Yeager's escort on the Thunderbirds' Good Will Tour around Central and South America. In 1953, we met the Thunderbirds in Mexico City, and I was introduced to Chuck Yeager. The first mistake I made was trying to carry his bag. He told me he was quite capable of carrying his own bag but asked me to keep an eye on him—and no surprises! I have never met anyone I enjoyed being with as much. He had just broken the sound barrier at Edwards AFB and set many speed records, but he never ran it into the ground. He was a perfect gentleman.

After the Good Will Tour, I didn't see Chuck Yeager for ten years. Then on one of my flights that included a midnight stop in Albuquerque, Yeager made a night dead-stick landing in a jet trainer after losing power forty miles east of Albuquerque. He landed "on the numbers" at the Air Base and turned off the runway just a few feet from us. He opened the canopy and matter-of-factly exclaimed, "Joe Martin and Jack Oliver, I last saw you on the Good Will Tour!" What an absolutely great person with such a great memory! We were so proud when he made General, and we have kept in touch for many years.

The night I met Chuck Yeager in Albuquerque, I was on a flight from Vandenberg AFB—the space and missile center—on the Pacific Coast. I had just finished a tour with the AEC (Atomic Energy Commission) in the Pacific, where we were testing atomic bombs, air dropped from B-29s or launched on a Thor Missile to various altitudes. I was a Major and a Satellite Operations Office at Vandenberg on orders to go to Hawaii to run the Satellite Tracking Station at Kaena Point. I had just spent a six-month tour with one of the greatest three-star generals I had ever met or worked with. Lt Gen Starbird was the commander of JTF-8, Department of Defense Joint Task Force, responsible for all B-29 air drops and missile/atomic bomb launches at Johnston Island. I was his FIC (Frequency Interference Officer) and Projects Manager, and we had loads of projects with AEC. I had an office on the *USS Hornet* Aircraft Carrier, our command post, for the air drops and on the *USNS Range Tracker* out of Fort Magu—near my old station at Vandenberg AFB. When we had to destroy an atomic bomb over the island, the General asked me to clear a path from the bunker, where he was holed up for the launch. I got my technicians from Fort Monmouth, New Jersey, and we opened up a pathway. There were highly radioactive fragments from the atomic bomb scattered all over the island. We cleared the path and called our cleanup folks at Pearl Harbor to come pick up the pieces.

General Starbird asked me to be his Aide at his next assignment at DCA (Defense Communications Agency). I visited with him in Washington, DC, after the tests, but my current Commanding General, General Bernard Schriever of Air Force Systems Command, said "NO," and he made me his commander of the Satellite Tracking Station at Kaena Point on Oahu, Hawaii. I was promoted to Lieutenant Colonel before arrival. General Schriever was an old Texas Aggie, and since I was an Aggie, he adopted me and my wife. He was both "Mr. Missile" and "Mr. Satellite" for the United States.

I spent four years in Hawaii at the Kaena Point Satellite Tracking Station. My experiences at Vandenberg AFB proved invaluable in managing the large Hawaiian tracking station with so many contractor civilian technicians on board. We tracked the highly classified satellites, read out data, and gave them appropriate commands to remain in space or to re-enter from space. Our sister group at Hickam AFB, Honolulu, Hawaii, caught the satellites as they returned from space and reeled them on board the C-119 and later the four-engine C-130 recovery aircraft. It was a successful four years, but it was time to return to the States.

I had met the Chief of Plans and Operations, Colonel Don Werbeck, when he was in charge of operations for the C-119 and C-130 recovery aircraft in Hawaii. He insisted that I come to Los Angeles to SAMSO Command (Space and Missiles and Satellite Operations) as his deputy. I did, and in six months he left for the AFSC Systems Command to work for General Bernard Schriever. I was promoted to full "Bird" Colonel and replaced Colonel— soon to be General—Werbeck as Chief of Operations for the Command. Not only was our office responsible for both the East and West Coast missile test ranges but also all missile and satellite operations at the ranges, including supporting NASA in their manned operations. General Werbeck soon got his second star and took over the Air Force Communications and Electronics Command at Scott Field, Illinois.

When General Werbeck left Systems Command, he insisted that I join DCA (Defense Communications Agency). They were responsible for DSCS II Defense Satellite Communications Systems, building over a dozen satellite receiving stations, strategically located all over the world. The stations had newly-developed 60-foot satellite dishes to control the twenty-four satellites in synchronous orbit and relay wideband and encrypted messages for our national defense forces. I moved to Fort Monmouth, New Jersey, to assist the Army in contracting, developing, and locating the new 60-foot terminals. DCA was footing the bills and served as oversight management. I was assigned as DCA's Chief East Coast Field Officer to monitor progress. We had three PL-313s (highly-paid scientific and professional civilian personnel) who had launched our response to the Russians first satellite. The three 313s, led by George Brown, adopted me since I was an old hand at satellites and knew their language. In a little over two years, we had the first 60-foot dish operating in Sunnyvale, California. In a year more, a contract was signed for the dozen dishes.

I was ready to retire as thirty years approached. I wrote a staff study recommending that the Army's COMSAT Organization (Communications Satellite Corporation) take over DCA's responsibly. It was approved, but very reluctantly, by Maj Gen Lewis Norman, my boss at Department Code 400, DCA. General Norman had worked with me for years, first at the Satellite Tracking Station in Hawaii and then at SAMSO in Los Angeles. General Norman was my hidden boss for many years because the Discoverer (code name *Corona*) Satellite Program actually belonged to the CIA (Central Intelligence Agency). I worked for the CIA, first at the Vandenberg Satellite Tracking Station in the Corona program, and then in Hawaii for four years. After I returned to SAMSO in Los Angeles, General Lewis Norman and the CIA made me the contact person for the CIA for all SAMSO offices. Even when I left SAMSO for DCA, I was not relieved of my responsibilities because we needed the communication ties with the Air Force Satellite Command and Control Systems. Upon my retirement in 1972, I asked my old boss, General Lewis

Norman, when I was to be debriefed. He looked me square in the eye and said sternly, "Never! Don't try anything funny." He gave me a neat handshake, wished me well, and we said goodbye. I came home to Texas.

I figured that I would not have the privilege and honor of working with any more General officers. I was wrong. I joined the National Sojourners at Fort Hood. It was an organization made up of active duty and retired officers and Masons from the Armed Forces. General Harvey "Jabo" Jablonski was in charge. He was a crackerjack, a retired Army two-star general, who had directed the US activity in Iran for ten years. He had enrolled in the US Military Academy in 1931 after having already graduated from Washington University, St. Louis, Missouri, in 1929. Under his leadership as team captain at West Point in 1933, Army had a 9-1 record and outscored their opponents 227 to 26. The Heroes of '76 is an affiliate, auxiliary organization of National Sojourners, and General Jablonski loved to take part in the ceremonies. He named my farm *Fort Oliver* and always held Hero Encampments on the farm. He insisted that my wife and I take part in activities at Fort Hood, which we did. We loved the Army, and I was proud of my old Regular Army commission. It opened many doors for us.

Until General Jablonski died in 1989, he made certain that I met and knew the Commanders and their staff officers at Fort Hood, as well as key Sergeants Major in III Corps and 1st Cavalry Division (Doug Hayes) and 2nd Armored Division (Don Thorpe). John Garth, our County Judge, loved it.

Yes, it was a privilege and honor to have been so fortunate to serve with such talented and dedicated General officers, not only in the Air Force but also the Army. I was selected to be the

Air Force representative on the Army's Retiree Council at Fort Hood consisting of 174 Texas Counties. I am on the council to this date. A three-star Army general still leads the council previously chaired by General Jablonski.

Some years after I retired from the Air Force, I was asked to run for Bell County Commissioner. I ran and subsequently won the election. In so doing, I found that a large segment of my commissioner's precinct was in Fort Hood. Many of my responsibilities had to with that Army Post, its active and retired people, and the thousands of civilian personnel working on the post and living in my precinct.

We have welcomed every new commanding general to Fort Hood, and along with our old County Judge, John Garth, ensured that they were friends of Bell County's Court. I knew of no one who didn't appreciate the relationship with our Bell County Court, which they often voiced publicly.

In talking about Major General Jablonski, the National Sojourners, and the Heroes of '76, it occurred to me that I had failed to mention one neat Army general. I met him at Schofield Barracks in Hawaii when he was a full Colonel and Chief of Staff for the 25th Infantry Division. He too belonged to our National Sojourners. About the time the 25th Infantry was being assigned to Vietnam, Colonel Frederick Weyand was promoted to Brigadier General and assigned as Deputy Commander of the 25th. He called me about a week before deployment of the 25th and asked me how he could go to Vietnam if he wasn't a Hero. It finally dawned on me that—because I was the Commander of Heroes of '76—he wanted me to assist in initiating him as a Hero. This we promptly did, and he left happy. A few years later, I noticed he had been appointed Chief of Staff of the Army and achieved the rank of four-star general.

Lieutenant Jack Oliver in Europe 1944
Bombardier-Navigator on the B-24 Liberator

⑤

MY CIVILIANS

It was an honor and a privilege to know and to personally work with some great civilians, not only at state but also at federal levels. I had known our US Congressman Bob Poage from the time I can remember. He was my dad's friend, and yes, my friend as well. He gave me the Principal Appointment to West Point in 1940 (for 1941), but I had a ruptured appendix and had to give it up. The next year, he gave me the Principal Appointment to Annapolis. They had a height minimum (five feet six inches) in those days, and I was only five feet four inches tall. We went through the mill, and I was ready to go when we found out about the height issue.

I was concerned but not heart broken. I went to Texas A&M. Dean Kyle, Texas A&M School of Agriculture, was my dad's old friend, and he adopted me at Aggieland. A&M's football stadium, *Kyle Field*, is named after him. When I left A&M to go into the Air Corps Aviation Cadets, I had not finished the semester. He ensured that I received credit for every class, and he later helped me secure many credit hours from my Air Force/Army education. I always went by to see him.

Our State Senator, Roy Sanderford, helped me get the appointments to West Point and Annapolis through Bob Poage, along with his friends and mine from my home town. Judge Kirk Evetts (District Judge), Judge W.A. Messer (County Judge), and our Bank Presidents (Judge Owen P. Carpenter and Roy Smith) all ended up as our lifetime friends, in and out of the service.

From my enlistment in November 1942 until the summer of 1948, the military pretty well determined my future on a day-to-day basis. I underwent my military training, was commissioned and rated, flew my fifty-three missions in WWII, worked as a line officer in the Army Air Corps, and attended Pilot Training in the Army's last class before we became Air Force. After graduating, I was assigned to Hensley Field, Dallas, Texas, to instruct reserve officers. Everyone had to have a ground job, and I had several, including Base Adjutant, Club Officer, and—oh yes—Public Relations Officer for Hensley Field. Remember, I went to General Nuckols' PIO School in 1946. Secretary Stuart Symington of the new Air Force decided to honor Hensley Field with an air show. He set up a great open house and scheduled the *Thunderbirds*, the Air Forces Acrobatic Team, for the festivities. I got a call from his office asking me to dream up a huge sign welcoming the public as they drove out of Dallas to Hensley Field. I came up with a large sign with the theme *Air Power is Peace Power*. He was elated and asked if he could use that theme during his tenure as our Air Force Secretary. He wrote me a great "thank-you" after the show, but I never heard from him again. At least I was honored.

After Hensley Field, I was too busy for a while flying B-29s and trying to work my way back into fighters to be involved very much in the civilian world. We moved to Kansas City and Central Air Defense and then on to Panama, which included flying freight all over Central and South America in the DC-3.

When we left Panama, we were assigned to LSU (Louisiana State University) to teach ROTC students and persuade them to consider becoming Air Force pilots. My old Colonel boss, the Commandant of Cadets, didn't like protocol, so guess who was elected to fill in for him! We had a retired three-star general, General Troy Middleton, who was the University President. We hit it right off during my first official visit to his office, representing my commander, the Commandant of Cadets. The Commandant simply would not attend any social events at the University and insisted that I go, with Miriam, to represent his office. It was unusual from a military perspective, but acceptable, to an extreme, by all parties.

I flew regularly out of Ryan Field, in North Baton Rouge, in our L-17 *Navion* aircraft, which we used to conduct two orientation flights for each LSU ROTC cadet. I came in late one night from Alexandria, when to my surprise, the State Governor of Louisiana landed right behind me and I was asked to wait to speak with him. The Governor hopped out of his plane, sent his pilot on to New Orleans, and asked me for a ride to the Governor's Mansion. Now my car was not a limousine, but he couldn't have cared less. We chatted all the way, and he then insisted that I come in for coffee before I went home. We had a nice visit, and I was invited back. General Middleton was elated that I knew the Governor.

My wife and I often went to the Faculty Club at LSU for Sunday brunch. It was a neat place to go with fine service. We met most of the department heads at LSU and most were congenial. The heads of the Education, Psychology, Sociology, and History Departments were very close to Miriam and me. They knew I helped the football players with their courses, along with my excellent Air Science Instructors, and they encouraged me to continue. One professor tutored Billy Canon for three years. Later Billy wrote and presented his own Heisman Trophy speech.

After graduating from LSU in Astronomy and finishing my duties as an ROTC Instructor, I went to Vandenberg AFB in California to learn the Air Force's classified space programs. After a couple of years, I was loaned to the AEC (Atomic Energy Commission) for the tests at Christmas and Johnston Islands. I met Werner Von Braun at Johnston Island when we had to destroy a nuclear warhead and missile on launch. It was close to the surface and made a mess on the island. Von Braun came down to Johnston to check on things. He was interested in "my" small group of Army Specialists who were finding, collecting, and storing the radiation debris. The nuclear bomb had been destroyed, and pieces were scattered all over Johnston Island. To this date, our team always felt Werner Von Braun was too lax in his approach, not only in regard to the crated or mounted nuclear bombs, but also the stockpile of nuclear waste we collected.

Von Braun eventually died of radiation sickness as did our three-star general commander and many other staff officers, who we thought were in the line of fire. Werner Von Braun was to continue in his advisory capacity for several years. I encountered him and the great American atomic scientist, Edward Teller, at Los Angeles in 1967–68, where I was promoted to full Colonel and assigned as the new Chief of Staff for Space and Missiles. I hadn't been in my new job long when I came to work one morning only to find Ed Teller sitting in my chair at my desk. He welcomed me to *my* office and then proceeded to tell me he had not only taken over my office but also my secretary for three or four days. He was on the President's Advisory Board for Space and Missiles, which often met at our Space and Missiles Headquarters. My predecessor had apparently arranged for them to utilize the office prior to his departure. Ed Teller reminded me that Werner Von Braun and Dr. Hans Mark, of the University of Texas and NASA-Ames Research Center, would also be using my office and secretary. Von Braun remembered me from Johnston Island, and I wished him well. He passed away a few years later. A great loss! We considered him the foremost rocket engineer in the world. Not many would question that.

When I left SAMSO in 1967, I was assigned to the East Coast Field Office as Director under Code 400 of the Defense Communications Agency.

The Army's Satellite Communications Agency provided an office for me and my secretary. I was not welcomed because my predecessor had stirred up the troops. Enough said. My secretary noted this and told me about three PL-313s appointed by Congress and assigned to the agency. They were the ones who worked with Werner Von Braun, the Director of the team that launched Explorer I, the first US Satellite. She invited them to come meet me for lunch. Two of them did so—Mr. George Sink and Mr. George Brown. When they found out I knew Von Braun and that he had used my office and was also with me at both Vandenberg AFB and Johnston Island, they adopted me! Eventually they helped the others to again work with our office. PL-313s are the highest level of scientific and professional civilian personnel and rank with Generals—and are treated accordingly.

The 313s suffered with me as they learned of all of our early losses in the Discoverer Satellite launches at Vandenberg as well as our experiences at Johnston Island with the destruction of the atomic bomb on launch and Von Braun's presence after the calamity. They loved him. The Satellite Communications Agency was tasked to develop, design, contract, and distribute some dozen 60-foot satellite communications dishes for DSCS II (Defense Satellite Communications Systems). I was from DCA and responsible for the satellites, terminals, and worldwide communication links. If only we could give credit—so greatly deserved—to all of those great civilian workhorses and contractors, so strategically located throughout the military services! But not let us of the military services fail to remember those great civilian educators from our Cradle Roll days through college and even civilian life—before and after our service tenures—that set us on the right courses in our lives!

As I close down my remembrances of all of my wonderful civilian contacts, I want to go back and thank Professor Ernest White of Mary Hardin Baylor for developing and nurturing my interest in the stars, astronomy, and celestial navigation. Thanks go as well to my first flight instructor, Mr. Coulter, of Coulter Field, Bryan, Texas, for believing in me when I wanted to be a pilot. Through his patience and understanding, he built the foundation for me to become a safe, lifetime pilot of fighters, bombers, transports and civilian planes. I retired to my "rocking chair" as an Octogenarian UFO, with a valid FAA License, having flown my own plane well after reaching eighty years of age.

I had traveled all over the world and our United States. But when I came home to Bell County, Texas, I found my own Bell County citizens to be the best civilians of all. They were dedicated to our County and State, loyal to a fault, yet operating with meager compensation—sometimes under antiquated conditions with a minimum of equipment and supplies. When I was persuaded to run for County Commissioner and began my campaign, my eyes were opened to the needs of the employees and the various departments. Our clerks, road crews, and deputy sheriffs operated on the lowest of salaries. Compensation was pitiful compared to other counties. There was no organized system to reward personnel. In short, our clerks, crews, sheriffs, and all others needed someone to champion their plight. Our new Judge and new Commissioners could not believe how financially bad Bell County was or the poor salaries paid Bell County employees. Something had to be done, and soon, for our citizens—*my* civilians.

We were not alone, we found out, when the Commissioners Court met with the Senior District Judge in Bell County. He had been a County Judge and readily understood our problems. The District Judge hired the County Auditor who was the watch-dog for the Commissioners Court. Judge Clawson picked Bert Liles as the Auditor to work with the Commissioners Court and he accepted the challenge. We soon had a new Sheriff, Dan Smith, who quickly realized the needs of his department. The Commissioners Court hired an engineer, Walter Neaves, who set up the Optional Road Law to run the county road crews. He also readily recognized the needed improvements in pay and equipment.

Slowly the department heads realized they had a leader in John Garth, our Judge, and the backing of District Judge Clawson. And our new Auditor turned out to be that special citizen (my civilian) who could work with the devil.

Things began to turn around, even with our first budget hearings. Our County and District Clerks were elated to see the change in the Court's attitude towards county employees. Finally, the people who would be the key to Bell County's growth and success would be recognized.

Flying County Commissioner and Co-pilot, Miriam

Jack and Miriam flew their four-place Mooney to State and National Commissioners Conferences all over the US while Jack was Bell County Commissioner (1979–91). They owned and operated the M-20C Mooney for twenty-five years. Mooney N1364W was maintained throughout that time by aircraft mechanic, "Sid" Sutton, in its hangar in Killeen, Texas.

6

YOUR COUNTY COMMISSIONER

Yes, after thirty years of military service and retiring from the Air Force in 1972, building a new home on our farm, buying cattle, re-fencing the farm, and becoming active with my wife in our community, I was asked to run for County Commissioner. Several leaders in our community, our church leaders, and two ministers of churches in Belton—my home town—asked me to consider tossing my hat into the ring. About this time I got a call from Roy Smith, President of the First National Bank in Killeen (adjacent to Fort Hood); Killeen Fire Chief Blondie Rucker; the retired Fort Hood Fire Chief; the Director of Civilian Personnel at Fort Hood; and two senior Sergeants—CSM Doug Hayes of the 1st Calvary Division and CSM Don Thorpe of the 2nd Armored Division. All of these individuals asked me to run for County Commissioner. Before I could turn around, I had the Superintendent of Public Schools in Killeen calling me, as well as the VFW, American Legion, the Retired Command Sergeants Major Organization chaired by Retired CSM Green—urged on by CSM Doug Hayes and CSM Don Thorpe—and Major General Ret. "Jobo" Jablonski. The General explained that two service men, albeit from other states, had run for County Commissioner and had lost miserably, even though they had retired from Fort Hood. Both CSM Hayes and CSM Thorpe had approached the General and asked him if he might call me, an old Bell County boy, born and raised locally, to consider running for Bell County Commissioner. General Jablonski was also a friend of the Killeen First National Bank President, Roy Smith. Before long I got a letter from SGM King of Fort Monmouth, New Jersey, who was a friend of Sergeants Hayes, Thorpe, and Green, plus several other retired NCOs at Fort Hood, including the III Corps Command Sergeant Major. It seems that SGM King and all of those sergeants were friends.

They had all heard that I was from Bell County, my dad having been Commander of the National Guard in Belton; that I had served in the Army for five years in World War II; had gone to Texas A&M; and had accepted a Regular Army Commission in 1947. They wanted to support a person of military background, but someone born and totally accepted in Bell County as the candidate for Bell County Commissioner.

I received all of their attention in 1977–78 just as I had finished my new home and extensive work on the farm. I was thinking of taking a long vacation with my wife and going to Hawaii or driving across Canada and going to see old WWII friends in the United States.

I was very active in the Belton Lions Club, and the ministers of the First Baptist Church and Church of Christ in Belton— both Lions in my old home town—pushed me hard to run for County Commissioner. When at first I refused, the Baptist minister reminded me that one "never stops serving." Afterwards, I explained to him that I had just served thirty years in the Air Force and had two Purple Hearts from WWII. He was not impressed and took me to see the Church of Christ Minister in Belton and their counterparts and lay-leaders in Killeen. He then took me to see the American State Bank President in Killeen who "quietly" promised to support me if I would run. His first and second vice-presidents also agreed to help. They are all friends to this day.

Well, I finally got out to Fort Hood to see our SGM Doug Hayes and SGM Don Thorpe. I thanked them, but reminded them that campaigning for office on Fort Hood wasn't allowed. They explained that I just didn't understand, and that they would show me how to run for a political office on the Army Post. After being escorted out of two or three places and being tutored by the III Corps Command Sergeant Major, we visited every sergeant major and first sergeant on Fort Hood plus every office supervised by a senior sergeant. It was a great experiment and they all meant well, but campaigning on Fort Hood could only be called an experiment. Yes, I believed the key personnel, civilian employees, and the senior non-commissioned officers ultimately voted for me, but the average soldier voted back home as did most of the officers.

I won the election, first the primary and then the run-off election. I was in for four years. My sergeants and the Army had a military man in office for the first time for Fort Hood. They received a two-for-one because John Garth was running for County Judge. He also won, and he was very patriotic and pro Fort Hood. Fort Hood now had two votes on the Commissioners Court, and they could pretty well count on two other commissioners, who had served in World War II. I served for twelve years—three four-year terms. Judge Garth served five terms.

Fort Hood's soldiers and civilian employees have had a great relationship with Bell County and all of its various offices for many years. Of all the things I have accomplished in my lifetime, I would definitely repeat my military service, but I enjoyed totally my twelve years as Bell County Commissioner, serving my friends and acquaintances in Bell County, Texas. It was an honor and a privilege. John Garth and his commissioners took a county that was broke and rundown—many said "mismanaged"—and made it into a great county, the envy of many of the big counties in the State.

But back to the campaign for Precinct 4 Commissioner.... Precinct 4 included a large area and lots of people in the 1970s. It covered all of Killeen and Fort Hood and all of Bell County from Bartlett and Holland to Youngsport, Maxdale, plus western and southwestern Bell County. It did not cover Harker Heights because it was in Precinct 2, supposedly to equalize the vote. Nothing could be further from the truth. Precinct 4 had sixty-nine thousand voters and Precinct 2 only twenty-nine thousand. Not one man, one vote by any means! Redistricting came up in 1980 and again in 1990 to equalize the vote between Precincts 2 and 4. The tide turned in 1990, and the precincts were fairly well equalized.

As hard as I worked on Fort Hood with my sergeants and civilian personnel friends, little was done there until precinct lines were redrawn in the early 1990s. I would be remiss if I failed to mention my wife Miriam and her part in my running for Bell County Commissioner. To this day, she claims it was her idea for me to run. In fact, I probably would not have run—even after so many people were encouraging me to do so—if it hadn't have been for Miriam's total commitment to our doing it. We lived twenty-five miles southeast of Killeen and Fort Hood where ninety percent of the voters in Precinct 4 lived. This meant that we were up at 5:00 AM on most mornings to be in Killeen at 6:00 AM. After a long day—some days extending until 9:30 or 10:00 PM—we fell into bed, only to repeat it again the next day. This went on for over a year. Yes, Miriam was dedicated and stuck by my side, walking every street and knocking on every door in the City of Killeen.

After several weeks of listening to our many new acquaintances and old friends and family, we were still having trouble tossing our hat into the ring to run for Commissioner. Then an incident at a Commissioners Court meeting involving the incumbent commissioners settled the issue. I received a call the next day from Roy Smith, President of the First National Bank in Killeen, asking me if I had now decided to run. The old commissioner had insulted a Killeen constituent and chased him out of the court room—with the TV cameras running. Mr. Smith pressured me for an answer to his question, "Are you going to run now?" I checked with my wife, who had heard it all, and we agreed that I should run. We both knew what this meant—a year or more of tireless activity. I called Roy Smith back and told him we would run and would contact the *Killeen Daily Herald* that day for an announcement.

We were pleasantly surprised when we went to see the Managing Editor of the newspaper, Ray Townsend, and his capable assistant and Editor of the paper, Jerry Skidmore. They were elated that we were running and insisted on introducing us to the staff.

It was time to locate a campaign headquarters, so we called an old friend Noel Spaulding and met him at the Cowhouse. He insisted on putting up a sign in front of the Cowhouse designating it as such. The next morning at a 6:00 AM meeting, Noel Spaulding had a campaign committee on board—Noel Spaulding, Slim Krewsom, Al Pierce, Louis Robinson, Benjy Norman, Joe Williamson, Lewis McClaren, and Bill McKinney. Louis Robinson was selected to write and/or review all news releases. He promptly went to work on our "free" newspaper announcement, with picture, for the *Killeen Daily Herald*. We had to be careful because our three opponents were from Killeen and we were from and lived in the east end of the precinct, about five miles east of Interstate 35.

We continued making the rounds of the precinct, walking the streets of Killeen, attending every city function, and putting daily notices in the Killeen paper with our theme "Take a new Twist, Vote Oliver!" The *Oliver Twist* was catchy and it caught on fast. We won the primary, top vote-getter of the four candidates. Now a run-off for the top two!

The old commissioner was out. He lost in the primary, as did one other candidate. I did not get over fifty percent of the vote, so I had to run against the next highest vote-getter. Our work was cut out for us because our opponent was a local boy, born and raised in Killeen. In the end, this was his downfall. He had a lot of friends in the city, but he never understood the Army and their needs as a community. Nor did he know or understand the Black community. He would quietly make derogatory comments about the history of African-Americans in Killeen, that there used to be a sign that cautioned Black people, "Don't let the sun go down if you are in Killeen—get out of town!" The Killeen city shops' foreman asked us to talk to their employees separately, which we did. All went well until my opponent stated that he was glad to see that there were no Blacks employed by the city! He missed one Puerto Rican employee whose mother was African-American. That employee told his Pershing Park Black Baptist Minister, R.A. Abercrombie, who then called me. I had been by to see him a week or two earlier, and he was non-committal. He was now fully committed to my election and offered his staff's and his congregation's help in my election as their Commissioner.

If it hadn't been for the retired military, civilian personnel on Fort Hood, those old dedicated sergeants, the Killeen school teachers—who liked my having a degree—the Killeen Fire Department and Volunteers, the Police Department of Killeen, the many small businesses, and yes, Pershing Park Baptist Church, we would not have won the election. The votes we gained from each of these dedicated groups gave us the votes needed to win. As I mentioned, our opponent was a Killeen boy. He used every trick to beat us, including removing our signs and placing ads in the newspaper with derogatory statements—which we had to spend much time and effort rebuffing later. Two days before the run-off election, his campaign placed an article in the *Killeen Daily Herald* stating that we were from East Bell County, that our interests were east of Highway 35, and that we would always vote against Killeen once we were in office. It went on and on, degrading me and my character, emphasizing that nothing good had ever come out of Holland, Texas, or east Bell County. I of course lived near Holland, and that was my address.

Needless to say, Sergeant Major Louis Robinson wrote a fine rebuttal to the article that degraded me and my platform. Rather, I should say he re-wrote my first effort at rebutting the article. It was a masterpiece. The next morning, another old Killeen friend of ours insisted that we go with him to his coffee clutch behind his store in Killeen. We didn't know that half the people there were my opponent's friends. We hadn't sat down before one of them popped off saying, "Well, here is Oliver from Holland, Texas, in east Bell County. Nothing ever good has come out of Holland, Texas!" A gentleman at our table, whom I recognized as Coach Leo Buckley, immediately jumped to his feet, red-faced and obviously upset. He looked the guy square in the eye and said: "I'm from Holland. I was raised there!" There was deadly silence. Coach Buckley was the most honored and revered coach Killeen had ever had. In fact, they had just named their new High School Stadium after him. The next day, Coach Buckley brought his entire athletic staff to coffee and announced, "We, my staff and I, are supporting Oliver!" The next day was the run-off election. I won the election. It was not by a landslide, but it was a victory. I served twelve years, and I'd do it all over again. It was an honor and a privilege to serve the people of Killeen and all of Precinct 4. They are the greatest people in Bell County.

The first thing that the new County Commissioners Court did was to re-evaluate our Bell County Youth Fair and their anti-quated facilities near Temple High School. We had just held the annual Youth Fair in a facility that was extremely degrading. It was pathetic! We had to get our kids out of the mud and those leaky, run-down buildings! John Garth fielded the idea of an Exposition Center, centrally located in Bell County, with a new up-to-date show barn for the kids. We appointed a county committee to draw up the plans, and it was finally decided to place the Center south of Belton on Loop 121 for easy access. A county-wide meeting was called, producing full county support. The Court quickly acted, effected a loan to build the facility, and bought the land. Youth Fair Association members were elected. Each member of the Commissioners Court appointed a member to the Board of Directors. I selected Bill Yowell of Killeen, who served as an active member for twenty-five years. The dome, often called Garth Dome, has provided an entertainment center from day one for Bell County Citizens.

I would be remiss if I did not cover some of the things that our Commissioners Court did, led by Judge John Garth. He was a crackerjack! He had the knack of looking into the future and then planning for it. He led us out of a hole financially. We used to call him "The poor little rich man." He came from a well-to-do family, but you would think every penny we spent or budgeted came out of his personal pocket. He was tight, but not unreasonably so. Over a period of years, we developed a personnel system for the county and a pay system to recognize our county employees. Our clerks, deputy sheriffs, and our county road crews were finally recognized and paid accordingly. And yes, with no increase in taxes. We also built a new jail, an Exposition Center for the citizens of Bell County, and began work on a new legal complex just outside of town—we were not to see it finished, but we certainly got it started. John Garth wanted a Bell County Museum, so we got one. He rebuilt the old Carnegie Library and hired a professional to run the museum. It was a great success. The Court established the Optional Road Law and hired an engineer to run the county road system for all of the commissioners.

It took a while for the individual commissioners to give up their precinct barns, their foremen, their county road crews, and their fiefdoms—their precincts. Under the Optional Road Law, the precinct commissioner becomes the equivalent of a small state representative, but on the county level. Often, in larger counties, the commissioner is responsible for as many constituents in his precinct as the state representative—with a lot of responsibilities.

I covered Precinct 4, which included all of Killeen and the main parts of Fort Hood. Having been in the Army in World War II and twenty-five years in the Air Force, I enjoyed being responsible for Fort Hood and its forty thousand soldiers. I attended their functions, parades and honors, not only for the III Corps but also the Post and the 1st and 2nd Divisions. Our county judge insisted that I welcome all new commanding generals, command sergeant majors, and other senior officers and non-commissioned officers.

After twelve years, my father and mother needed my attention, so I did not run for a fourth four-year term. I still attend the Commissioners Court on a regular basis and support them. I continue to be a member of the 174-county Army Retiree Council as an associate member. Nearing eighty-seven years of age, I realize the time is rapidly approaching for me to step down. If so, I will miss it all.

I do believe that my two ministerial friends (and pastors) were correct in their belief that "one never stops serving." I have been particularly impressed by our current county judge and his staff of four commissioners. One and all have displayed this conviction that "one never stops serving" his fellow man. Our Commissioners Court, in this year of our Lord, 2011, can be proud of their unselfish interest in serving their constituents and Bell County as a whole. We in Bell County can rest easy in that we have this leadership. May they continue to be as dedicated as we, the old court, were in looking after Bell County. I think they will, and I can fade away, as has all of my Bell County Court of the 1980s and 1990s. I am a Bell County boy, born and bred here in the shadow of the Bell County Courthouse. What an honor it has been serving my Belton people and all of Bell County! I feel certain that the Good Lord will continue to bless and keep us all. Amen.

Jack and his Mooney N1364W

⑦

FLYING PART I

I had always wanted to be a pilot. We lived under the lighted airway from San Antonio to Dallas. Day and night, airplanes flew over our home. When I was just a kid, I lashed a long, one-by-sixteen inch board laterally to my coaster wagon and tried to fly off of the calf shed. I crashed!—small wonder I wasn't killed. I had great dreams of flying, even like Superman. I finally met an old pilot from Belton, our own Elmer Reed. He would let me sit in his airplane, but he wouldn't take me up unless my folks approved—and they never did!

When I went to A&M College of Texas in 1942, I found out that Mr. Coulter, of Bryan's Coulter Field, gave aircraft training flights. I was too busy with my courses and my corps of cadet activities in my first semester. However, in my second semester, I started riding my bicycle to Coulter Field and asking him to give me lessons to be a pilot. After two or three trips to see him, he finally agreed to let me fly—if I paid as I flew. I agreed because I had saved my farm money all along.

Mr. Coulter had an old Interstate Aircraft *Cadet* trainer with a tail skid. The aircraft was somewhat modern in that it had brakes on the main gear. My first hour in the cockpit did not involve flying. It was a busy lesson on learning to accelerate the engine just enough to raise the tail skid so I could apply brakes and turn the aircraft. He repeated often: "Learn it well! If you raise that tail too much and mess up my prop, you had better start running—and never stop, because if I catch you, you will never be able to even try flying!"

I believed Mr. Coulter and never forgot his warning. He let me fly solo after eight or nine hours. Then came airwork flying for another ten or more hours. I was hooked. I was a pilot! About this time, in the fall of 1942, I became eighteen years of age and enlisted in the Army. My dad swore me into the Enlisted Reserve Corps. He thought I would go into advanced ROTC the next year and become an Infantry Officer.

Little did my dad know that I was hooked on flying, and nothing could stop me from going into the Army's Aviation Cadet Program to be a pilot! A&M Cadet Corps SGM Dunbar, under the Corps Commandant of Cadets, allowed me to go to Houston with a load of sophomore cadets to take the exams for aviation cadet training. I passed the exams for pilot, navigator, and bombardier. I was thrilled. I could be a pilot. But, not so fast! The examiner said I was not to be a pilot, but rather a navigator! My arguments proved futile, and when it came down to take-it-or-leave-it, I agreed to be a navigator. I was sent back to A&M to finish the semester and await a class assignment. Before the semester was over, I had a class date and received orders to go to San Angelo, Texas, for Bombardier-Navigator training.

This was the first class of "Bombagators" where one learned to be a Bombardier *and* a Navigator. I graduated October 23, 1943, and was ordered to Salt Lake City for officer crewing of a B-24 Bomber. My desire to become a pilot was placed on the shelf for now. The second Great War was on, and I was now a member of a combat crew training for combat. That was all that mattered. Our crew of ten men was formed. We trained in the B-24, and early in the New Year of 1944, we departed for Italy. In six months, I had flown fifty-three combat missions, awarded two Purple Hearts, and then allowed to come home.

I was asked to go to Tucson, Arizona, to Davis-Monthan Field and set up a ground school for a new set of Navigators and Bombardiers to crew a new tactical Bomber—consisting of the best characteristics of the B-24 and B-17. After three months in the winter of 1944, the program was cancelled because the new B-29 bomber was coming along faster than they had imagined. The school was closed, and I was sent to San Marcos, Texas, to teach Navigators. Shortly, that field closed, and we were sent to teach Navigators at Ellington Field near Houston, Texas. Then Ellington was closed after a few months. The war was over in the fall of 1945 and the Air Corps was cutting back fast.

Several of us were promised an opportunity to go to the Army's Pilot Training School on our return from combat. We were repeatedly assured that we were still on the list when a class opened up. They shipped us off to Amarillo to give basic training to thirty thousand draftees for ninety days so they would be able to receive Veterans Administration benefits. This was one of the greatest programs ever fielded for our Country's future. These guys then went to school, built homes, and created jobs. Great! After six months, we closed the base and sent the trainees home. We of the cadre were dispersed all over the remaining Army Air Corps bases. I was sent to Keesler Field at Biloxi, Mississippi, and assigned as a Public Information Officer. I also ran the base newspaper.

After ninety days, I was sent to PIO (Public Information Officer) school at Selma, Alabama. I checked to see what would happen if my pilot class date came in. I was assured that I would be notified. The PIO School was a great experience and led by General William Nuckols. General Nuckols was later appointed by General Matthew Ridgeway as Director of Information, United Nations Command (Advance) in Korea, soon after the military armistice conferences began in July 1951.

Nuckols was fantastic. We learned a lot, from writing, to speaking, to supporting the Army Air Corps and its variety of missions. My orders for a pilot training class (Class 47C) finally came in, the first class in over two years. I could not get back in time because we were on a trip with Gen Nuckols to New York City. But the Army kept its word, and I was assigned to the next pilot class (Class 48A)—training in 1947 and graduating February 1948.

At the end of WWII, eight hundred of us—navigators, bombardiers, and engineer officers—were promised a chance to go to pilot training. After over two years, two hundred were left to attend Class 47C and two hundred Class 48A. They also added eighty aviation cadets to our class, the first cadets in several years. This was good, but bad for the student officers, who were treated even worse than the cadets. During the course of our training, it seemed to me that all they wanted to do was *washout* (eliminate) most of the pilot trainees from pilot training.

We were the last class to fly the *Rag-Wing*, the nickname for the bi-wing Stearman aircraft. It was a great little acrobatic plane and used extensively by the Navy and Air Corps. In primary training in the Stearman, we were put through the wringer. Many officers washed out! Then we moved to basic training in the T-6 Texan, a great instrument trainer used by the Army in advanced training during WWII. To this day, I think my training on instruments in the T-6 Texan saved my life many times. After Basic Training at Randolph Field, the students scheduled for multi-engine advanced went to Barksdale Field, and we single-engine pilots went to Williams Field at Chandler, Arizona. We were promptly checked out in the famous P-51 Mustang but continued night and weather instrument training in the T-6 Texan. Note the designation "P" in P-51. P stood for "Pursuit" in the Army, and we were Army student pilots. In the fall of 1947, a new law was passed forming the US Air Force. Several of us— yes, just 10—were picked to fly the Army's first jet fighter used operationally, the P-80 jet. It became the F-80 in 1948, and all of us were transferred to the Air Force. In spite of the law, two of us—Bill Shadel and myself—were tendered Regular Army commissions in December 1947. My commissioning document was dated December 31, 1947.

Most of those flying the F-80 were sent to jet fighter units. Two of our men were Joseph McConnell, the leading F-86 *Sabre* ace in Korea with sixteen victories, and Cecil Foster, who had nine victories to his credit. I car-pooled with these two officers in pilot training, and I readily admit they could fly rings around me—and I thought I was a pretty good pilot!

Upon graduation from pilot training at Williams Field, I was assigned with Cecil Foster to check out reserve pilots at Hensley Field, Dallas, Texas, in the F-80 jet. The program was subsequently cancelled, and we trained reserve officers in the T-6 Texan and the twin-engined C-45s, T-7s, and T-11s. In a few months, Cecil Foster was assigned to jets in Alaska and later went to Korea. I was to remain a few months as Base Adjutant at Hensley Field. Shortly, I received orders to go to Castle AFB, Merced, California, to fly B-29s because I was triple-rated—pilot, bombardier, and celestial navigator. I had also previously had a tour in B-24s in Italy in WWII. My dreams of being a jet fighter pilot were dashed.

After flying the B-29 in the winter of 1948–49, I found that that old bird was built for the crew. It was a great airplane, but my days were numbered in the B-29.

After I had completed my stint as a copilot in the B-29, I was sent to MacDill AFB in Tampa, Florida, to check out in the B-29 as first pilot and to be assigned my crew. I finished the transition course, graduated with honors, and had fallen in love with the big *Superfortress*.

The day after I graduated, a SAC Headquarters Standardization Board pilot showed up two days late to ride with several of us just after we completed the course. I was still awaiting a pickup from Castle, so I agreed to a ride. Another flight in the B-29, even with the Stan Board, was welcomed. The following morning at 4:00 AM, we met at the flight line. It was raining and the weather was nasty, but in SAC, you flew, whatever. The Stan Board pilot insisted that I climb a seventeen-foot ladder, with all my equipment on, and enter the cockpit from the top hatch. At the top rung, I slipped and fell back the full seventeen-plus feet to the ground, landing on my back. It was bad, and I was rushed to the hospital with a fractured back. That was the end of any Stan-Board ride and flying the B-29.

After my return to Castle AFB, I was reassigned to March AFB, the home of the First Fighter Wing. They were transitioning into the F-86. I was back on flying status as a pilot, but there were no openings to fly the F-86.

The Commander of the First Fighter Wing knew I was a Regular Army Officer (transferred to the Air Force) and asked me to be a squadron adjutant until I could be moved into the jet fighter. I *reluctantly* agreed. He then offered to let me fly the P-51 Mustang if I would tow targets for the jet-fighter pilot trainees. He also told me that I could have a P-51 to go anywhere in the United States, once a month, if I accepted. Now I *readily* agreed! It was great flying. Everywhere I went, from the smallest civilian field to the largest military and commercial airports, the P-51 was admired and respected because of its role in WWII. I never had anyone attempt to mar the P-51, steal anything, or even try too. What struck me most was the silence, and deep respect, whether they were age six or sixty-six. They would touch the P-51 like it was a god. That was the greatest flying I ever had in the Air Force. I never got to fly the F-86 because the First Fighter Wing was disbanded, and by then—as the Wing/Base Adjutant—I had to cut the orders disbanding the Wing and disbursing its squadrons around the United States. I was sent to Kansas City as part of the cadre to organize the Central Air Defense. There I flew DC3s and C-45s. There was nothing else.

In the military, you can't shake being an adjutant (administrative officer). I was assigned as Base Adjutant at Central Air Defense. Once we got settled, the Deputy Commander picked me to be his Secretary for the command's Promotion Board. He was President. When we completed board proceedings, I was expecting to go back to Lt Col Shoup as Headquarters Adjutant and I mentioned it to Gen Robinson. He flatly told me that I was staying in the headquarters, and that I was to be the new Director of Officer Personnel. I reminded him that I was a First Lieutenant, not yet a Captain, and the position called for a field grade officer.

He ignored me, told me to clear out my desk at Lt Col Shoup's headquarters unit, and to report for duty as Personnel Officer for the command. I quickly found out why I was given the assignment—I was a WWII veteran with fifty-three missions and two Purple Hearts. It would be my duty to identify any and all of the officers in the command, Central Air Defense, who had not been overseas in WWII. I was to line them up, with their aircraft preference noted, and send them to the Korean War. We got most of them, and I was not popular. But I also kept putting my name down on every list of officer pilots to go to Korea. Gen Robinson liked this at first, but would remove my name from every list.

Then the General grew tired of the fact that I put my name on the lists, and he began giving me hell! After a period of time, he called me in and announced that he had my assignment overseas. I asked him what I would be flying in Korea. He looked at me and said blankly: "You're not going to Korea. You're going to Panama and you're going to fly the DC-3 Gooney Bird." I nearly died. I just knew I had to fly combat in Korea if I were ever to be promoted again in the Air Force. Gen Robinson was not deterred and proceeded to tell me what I would be doing in Panama. He had it all arranged with the commanding general of Caribbean Command in Panama and the chief of all Air Force personnel. "Oliver," he said, "you are going to Panama, Central and South America, to change all Air Force personnel's MOS (Military Occupation Specialist) designations to AFSCs (Air Force Specialty Code), the new Air Force designations"!

In a week I was on orders to go to the Air Force's Personnel and Assignments Command at Lowry AFB in Denver, Colorado, to learn and become a Qualification and Assignments Officer for the Caribbean Air Command in Panama, covering all of Central and South America.

We arrived in Panama on May 17, 1952, and after getting my family settled in their quarters at Albrook AFB, I was taken up to Caribbean Air Command and briefed on my assignment. Then I was told that I would be given a second lieutenant as my co-pilot and a new buck-sergeant flight engineer. We were to fly to every country in Central and South America, brief all Air Force personnel on the new AFSC designations, and change every person's MOS to an Air Force Specialty Code. To top it off, we were to examine everyone's proficiency level in Spanish and make appropriate entries on their records. I was quietly told to not fail anyone on the Spanish exam.

We had to get acquainted as a crew, get a check-out in the DC-3 Gooney Bird, get briefed on Central and South American flying, secure applicable clearances for the foreign countries, and gather what little weather and landing field information was available. My co-pilot had never been in a twin-engine plane, and the engineer had never been in a DC-3, much less served as a crewmember on an airplane. In a week, Caribbean Command considered us ready to go, cut orders for us to depart for Mexico City, handed us the appropriate clearances, and sent us on our way—yes, in only one week!

Lieutenant Jack Oliver in front of his flak-damaged B-24
(Little De-Icer) in Italy 1944

8

FLYING PART II

I was fairly well checked-out in the DC-3, the Gooney Bird, as I had been flying it regularly out of Kansas City and the Olathe Naval Air Station—before and during the great Missouri River floods of 1951. For many weeks, I hauled chemicals and DDT in fifty-gallon drums—plus, of course, Central Air Defense personnel, who needed a fast flight in and about the command—from one end of the Missouri River to the other. About this time, I became a Senior Pilot—with over two thousand hours of pilot flying time—and held an instrument flight all-weather Green Card, so I was able to file and sign my own clearances. This worked out particularly well in South and Central America but also for the times I was able to drop into the States.

We finished our local check-out in the DC-3 in record time and were given a thorough command briefing. We were informed that we were to brief and service every one of the Air Attachés' offices at the US Embassies in every country and make their conversions to AFSC from MOS. We were reminded that we were to administer the Spanish exam—but pass everyone! We also were given a short course in diplomatic relations, as they applied to each country. This was probably the most important phase of our briefings; and it came in handy, from offering cigarettes to giving gifts—different in each country.

There were Air Force Missions in every Central and South American Country. Some had staffs of four or five people, others up to fifty, such as in Brazil. Oh yes, Brazil did have Portuguese as their language, but it was the only one. So we just faked our way, and by the time we hit Brazil, we had Portuguese language exams anyway. All of the Mission and Air Attaché folks were English-speaking, so we had no problems.

Our first country was Mexico, and we hit our first mile-high destination and operations base, Mexico City—about the same elevation as Denver, Colorado. All went well, with no troubles, even though we expected some from the Air Attaché, Embassy folks. We finished up in four or five days and had a chance to visit the pyramids north of Mexico City. Then we filed clearances and received permission to enter Guatemala. Guatemala had a large Air Force Mission, with nearly all of the Air Force special-ties, including maintenance, supply, personnel, crew-members, and instructors. This took time, and we remained over a week. Everyone worked with us and even showed us some of the local sights including several noted volcanos in the country.

We picked up a Geodetic Survey Air Force pilot who was map-ping the coast lines of Guatemala and the other Central American Countries. We assisted him with his record conversions and became friends for life. Later, he became our neighbor in the fam-ily quarters in Panama, checked me out in the B-26 to tow targets for the Army, and gave us great information in dealing with the other Central American countries. E.C. Chappelle not only knew Central and South America well, but he ended up in Washington, DC, flying as pilot for Vice President Lyndon B. Johnson in the T-39. Later in civilian life, he was able to line me up with a four-place Mooney aircraft with retractable gear and a constant speed prop, which we owned and flew for twenty-five years. We met other Air Force flyers and personnel in Panama, as well as others serving many countries, who proved to be great friends with us in our service in the Air Force during and after departing Panama in 1955.

During our stay in Guatemala, we had no trouble with the DC-3, and our crew members were getting to know the Gooney Bird pretty well. Next, we were briefed and then filed for Nicaragua (Managua), Honduras (Tegucigalpa), and on to Costa Rica (San Jose). These were small detachments, so we could only stretch our stay to three days, even if we wanted a day or two to tour the country. Nicaragua, El Salvador, and Honduras had reasonably good runways, but no navigational flight aids. Costa Rica didn't have a landing field available in San Jose, so we used the country's Polo Field. The DC-3 could just make it in. After Costa Rica, we went back to Panama for a week of debriefings on Central America and also spent a couple of days briefing for South America. We then left for Quito, Ecuador, at nine thousand feet altitude, and on to Lima, Peru, which was at sea level. An Ecuadoran pilot at that stop had gone to pilot training with me and my buck sergeant engineer was from Quito, so we stayed a couple of extra days before going on to Lima, Peru.

We filled up on *langosta* in Ecuador. They are lobsters without claws, but just as good. Lima, Peru, was a wonderful city/country. We were welcomed with open arms. Lima had a large Air Force detachment and Air Attaché. We went right to work, but were soon introduced to *Pisco Sours*, as had every visiting flyer over the years. It was a wicked little drink of pisco liquor (about 150 proof), shaken ice, lime juice, egg whites, simple syrup, and bitters. So smooth! A person is not aware until he has fallen victim, having eased down three or four, because they are so good. Of course, that took care of a tour of the town—you slept! After a week in Peru and buying beautiful crystal sets, we went to Santiago, Chili. We fell in love with Chili. It was a beautiful country of beautiful people—a combination of French, Spanish and Portuguese. They were so friendly, as were our Air Force Mission folks and the Air Attaché's people. The beautiful vineyards made you think of Germany or France. The folks from Chili even had a navy and were a proud people. We really liked them. But in a week, we had finished our work.

Of course, in Chili we also went shopping for silver, silver service sets, candelabras, and more, departing with lots of presents for our wives and families when we got back home. Next, it would have been La Paz, Bolivia, but we were not cleared to take off at thirteen thousand feet. So it was across the Andes Mountains to Buenos Aires (BA), the home of an old Dictator, Peron. Buenos Aires was a beautiful country with a great airfield and a large staff of Air Force people. And of all things, we ran across an old Air Force friend and Medal of Honor winner, who was the Air Attaché in Argentina. I had gone to the Air Corps Public Relations School with him in Selma, Alabama, in 1946 (before pilot training). Argentina was a great cattle country and we ate some of the best beef we had ever tasted. My Air Attaché friend briefed us on our planned flights to Montevideo, Uruguay, Asuncion, Paraguay, and our flight route home through Uruguay and Paraguay, with a quick stop in Lima, Peru.

We returned to Panama for a week's rest, to see our families, and report our progress to the Caribbean Air Command (CAirC) personnel folks. It also gave us an opportunity to get that great old DC-3 *Triple-Nichol* checked over and cleared for that long flight to Rio de Janeiro and to check on diplomatic clearances. This was important because Ecuador, Columbia, and Venezuela were not on good terms with one another. Fortunately, there were no problems with US relations. Our first stop out of Panama was Columbia, and we were able to visit my dad's cousin, Colonel Al Key, who was Mission Chief. Al Key was one of the first B-17 pilots in the Pacific in WWII. But Al and his brother, Fred, were more famous for their single-engine Curtiss Robin airplane *Old Miss*, which hangs in the Smithsonian Museum in Washington, DC, right next to *The Spirit of St. Louis* and the *Wright Flyer*. In the mid '30s they broke many records, including the length of flight (more than twenty-seven non-stop days and nights) and air-to-air refueling contacts (over one hundred air-to-air contacts with their refueling pilots).

After Columbia, we flew to the Dutch East Indies Island of Curacao to ease diplomatic relations (vis-à-vis entering) from another country (Netherlands) and not Columbia. It worked. We had a nice visit in Venezuela. They had a large mission at the capitol, Caracas, and at Lake Maracaibo. At Maracaibo, we got to visit with a Venezuelan pilot with whom I had gone to pilot training in 1947 at Randolph AFB, Major Luis E. Finol, who later became General Finol and Commander of the Venezuelan Air Forces. He is now retired and lives in Florida. From Venezuela, we were required to fly to Trinidad and Jamaica before we could proceed south to Brazil, once more for diplomatic reasons. But we encountered no significant problems in any countries—they all welcomed us. We took on fuel and obtained clearances to Belem, Brazil, on the Amazon River. Then we were cleared to Rio de Janeiro, capitol of Brazil, some eight hundred miles away.

About half way to Rio, our trusty DC-3 "swallowed" a valve in one of the pistons. We had to shut down the engine and feather the prop at eight thousand feet. We nurtured old *Triple-Nichol* to Rio, arriving at pattern altitude, which was typically fifteen hundred feet. We took care of our Portuguese-speaking friends with AFSCs versus MOS and helped our little engineer change the engine. After ten days, we had the engine going—all checked out fine—and we took off for Cochabamba, Bolivia, at ninety-five hundred feet, the entry to La Paz, Bolivia (thirteen thousand feet).

A senior Air Force NCO assisted with services at our stop in Cochabamba, and we took care of his MOS-AFSC conversion plus the quick Spanish test. He was very helpful and refused— thankfully!—to fully gas up our DC-3. He cautioned that our DC-3 should have just enough fuel to make Lima Peru from La Paz. There were no services available at high-elevation La Paz. We were told we would be briefed by Col Whatley, the Mission Chief, on the appropriate takeoff procedure. Unfortunately, the Colonel was visiting Lima and Panama and was not due back for a week. There was no one there to talk to that night.

When I got up early the next morning, I went down for breakfast in the restaurant. Low and behold, there was McCarthy—an Aggie geologist—of Houston's Shamrock Hotel, with his two pilots having breakfast! I had met him two years before at a Texas A&M Aggie Muster. I answered his question about why I was there and met his crew—two ex-marine Gooney Bird pilots. I was saved! They told me how to take off in the naturally-aspirated DC-3 from the thirteen thousand foot runway—carefully, with total control, and no inputs from the engineer or co-pilot! The key was a lean fuel mixture, no-flaps for 8,000 feet, then just twenty-five percent flaps with the tail up, letting the bird fly off at 12,500 to 13,000 feet. It was also important to avoid abrupt control movements, not add fuel or freight—not anything at La Paz!—and with luck, safely on to Lima.

Did I say we converted the La Paz bunch from MOS to AFSC? Yes, we did, except for Col Whatley. He could wait for a trip to Panama. It would be a long time before we returned to La Paz, Bolivia. We picked up a couple of stragglers in Lima and left for Panama. In six months, we had covered all Missions, Air Attachés, and their personnel from Mexico City through all of Central America and South America. *Triple-Nichol* did a great job for us.

My lieutenant became assistant base operations officer and was promoted to First Lieutenant. He briefed every flight from then on to Central and South America regions. Our little flight engineer finally made Staff Sergeant (SSgt) and then Tech Sergeant (TSgt) and engineered the base commander's B-17.

Yours truly reported to the Chief of Personnel for Caribbean Command. He patted me on the back and sent me to Albrook AFB, Panama, as Base Adjutant and OIC (Officer in Charge) of Officer Personnel. The previous occupant of that position had been air-evacuated to Washington, DC, due to a health problem, and I was given his job. He never returned. I served out my three years there.

Until I rotated back to the States in 1955, I continued to fly, primarily on long trips for the Command in the DC-3 throughout Central and South America. I also regularly flew four T-33 jet trainers that belonged to Columbia and towed targets for the Army in the B-26. I was kept busy.

In 1953, the Air Force decided to conduct a Good Will Tour around Central and South America, featuring the jet Thunderbird

Acrobatic Team and the great test pilot Chuck Yeager. Yeager spotlighted the show at every country visited. The following is my story about Yeager.

CHUCK YEAGER

I was the Base Adjutant at Albrook Field in the Canal Zone 1952–55, when our fledgling Air Force decided to host a Central and South American Good Will Tour, focused around the Air Force Thunderbird Team of F-86s and one Chuck Yeager. Yeager was the Air Force's most renowned test pilot, who had not only exceeded the speed of sound but had also accumulated a host of other accomplishments. The Caribbean Air Command/Albrook Field Personnel Office was given the responsibility as on-site chaperons for the tour. All of the staff that could be spared were assigned duties and were also appointed to serve as escorts to the tour's dignitaries. I was assigned to Chuck Yeager to answer his beck-and-call since I had been in the 1st Fighter Wing and had flown the P-51 and P-80. We got along just fine, except that you didn't carry Chuck Yeager's bag or anything else, but rather just accompanied him and enjoyed his company. He was one neat guy whom you could never get ahead of. He was always up, out, and gone before your feet hit the floor. The more I tried to help him, the less I could do. If you were with him in a group of people, he had the knack of making each and every person feel that only he or she was getting Yeager's attention. When we got to Santiago, Chili, the Command General realized that we did not have our formal uniforms for a scheduled shindig to be held in Buenos Aires. Since I was the Adjutant and Base Protocol Officer, the General wanted me to go back to Albrook in his B-17 and get everyone's uniforms with all the proper accouterments. But how would it be possible to get Chuck Yeager's escort and aide away from him? Realizing the General's dilemma, I requested that I be allowed to ask Chuck if I could be relieved, to which the General reluctantly agreed. When I told Chuck the predicament, I was relieved of whatever duty I had, given a swat on the back—along with countless thanks for my company—and loaded on that B-17. Chuck flew the F-86 solo aircraft at each show and in every capitol. What a fantastic flyer! When I left, I asked Chuck if it would be okay with him if I stayed at Albrook rather than return to Buenos Aires, since I was the Base Adjutant and nobody was left to look after things. He went straight to the Base Commander and informed him of his approval of my request. "What a guy!"

I did not see Yeager again for several years—nearly ten years. I was on a late-night cross-country in a T-Bird out of Vandenberg AFB. I landed at Albuquerque to refuel and to visit that old Base Commander from Albrook who was the Sandia National Laboratories Base Commander—or whatever AEC called the position back then. We were visiting and sitting on the tail-gate of his old pickup when the AO (Air Officer) came running out exclaiming: "Colonel, we've got a flameout in a T-33 forty miles east. The pilot said he wanted no emergency support, he would call when on final, and that he was turning everything off to save his battery." Before the pilot killed the aircraft's power, the AO quickly asked him if he could give his plane number and his name. The pilot gave the requested tail number and added as he signed off, "Pilot and soul occupant is Chuck Yeager." The AO asked Colonel Martin if he should get a fire truck and air police out there. The Colonel said, "No, just have them stand by!" Several minutes later, some landing lights flashed about a half mile out on final approach and then went out. That AO was anxious, but Col Martin said, "Relax!" It wasn't long afterwards that we heard the tires squeak as they touched the runway. A moment later, that T-Bird turned off at the center taxiway, rolled up to within twenty feet of our pickup tailgate where we were sitting, bowed gently—as if in salute—when the brakes were tapped, and then up came the canopy. Now mind you, Yeager had just *dead-sticked* that T-33 in from nearly forty miles out and rolled it right up to our pickup!

That's not all. I'm certain almost everyone has heard of Yeager's keen wit, his cleverness, his power to reason, and his memory that we all wish we had. And to perform this feat at midnight, in a pitch-black situation, over mountains! And the first thing he said was: "Martin and Oliver, what a welcoming party! Don't think I've seen either of you since South America on the Good Will Tour." Of the thousands of people he met on that tour, and of all the many more people since, he still remembered not only our last names but our first names as well. What a fantastic person! What a privilege to have known this fine and wonderful man and to have been able to do something for him when he has done so much for so many! With sincere respect, I remain "Jack" Oliver, USAF retired, his most humble servant.

I did not see Chuck again for several more years.

P-80 Shooting Star group picture
"The Chosen Ten"
(Jack is on far left, first row)

⑨

FLYING PART III

When I was assigned to Panama by General Robinson, I felt my Air Force career was doomed to flying Gooney Birds and being an administrative officer. I couldn't have been more wrong. New avenues opened up every day, but I didn't realize it for a long time. The first thing about flying the Gooney Bird (DC-3) in Central and South America was that you had long, boring legs to fly. Wrong! I had registered to brush up on my Spanish with the University of Maryland that had a contract with our Command (CAirC) for college courses. The University of Maryland was a land-grant school like Texas A&M, so A&M accepted every hour and credit. Also, the University of Maryland gave me several hours of credit for my military schools which A&M readily accepted as well. In three years, I had taken over sixty hours and had over ninety-three hours on the books at A&M. One day I received a letter from Pinky Downs at A&M asking if I wanted an Aggie senior ring—"Send $250 cash!" I did so, and by return mail, I received my A&M senior ring.

Oh, by the way, taking Spanish at the University of Maryland gave me the nine hours of foreign languages required for a degree from the University of Maryland or Texas A&M College. They even gave me nearly full credit for attending the Air Force

Personnel Qualification and Assignment course at Lowry Field and for the six months that I was converting everyone's MOS to AFSC. I was hooked. I took every college course I could to build up hours and studied constantly on those long DC-3 flights. But what about being *stuck* in the DC-3 Gooney Bird?! That was okay too because I was building up time—lots of it—as a Senior Pilot and Instructor Pilot. Things started to happen because of my old pilot skills and having been one of the first to fly the new jet, the F-80 fighter. My P-51 experience towing targets for our F-80 and F-86 pilots to practice gunnery also helped—we called the targets "rags." Well, the United States made a contract with Columbia to buy four T-33 jet trainers, which were essentially stretched versions of the F-80. But by the time they were delivered to Panama for pickup, Venezuela and Columbia were at great odds.

The Caribbean Air Command was ordered to hold the T-33 jets and keep them in flyable storage. There were only two pilots in the entire command that had ever flown the F-80. One was a colonel, our Director of Material for the command, and he had only received a couple of orientation rides. I had not only been checked out in the F-80 jet but had also logged several operational hours. I had also been assigned as an instructor in the P-80. Therefore, I was ordered by the Chief of Staff for CAirC Operations to keep the T-33s in flyable storage, which meant a flight per month in each plane. I was elated because I could build up my jet time. But the T-33 was *not* the F-80. It had a new Bendix fuel metering device, and any aspiring Instructor Pilot had to have at least ten hours of instructor training in the T-33 to be so designated. The Chief of Operations called me in to announce that I was going to the States to get checked out, but Training Command now insisted on thirty hours, not ten! The Chief asked me if any of my buddies could cover me with the ten hours anticipated earlier. I called one of the ten pilots I had checked out with in the P-80 (F-80) in the old Army days. He suggested that I phone "Bob" McCully, who was Chief of Training for F-86Ds at Tyndall Field. I called Bob and asked if he could help since the F-86D pilots had to get ten hours in the T-33 before they could go into F-86s. He obtained permission from his Command to run me through, if no questions were ever asked. Within a few days, I had flown to Tyndall in a DC-3, completed the ten-hour course plus a couple of additional hours to qualify as an Instructor Pilot in the T-33, and was then picked up by a DC-3 from Panama.

Even though the T-33s belonged to Columbia, our Command Chief of Operations and all of his wheel buddies were required to have a jet ride with a qualified Air Force Instructor Pilot. This all had to be logged in their personal log book and Form 5, their record of Air Force Flying. This went on for two years. Then I had to check out the Columbian pilots when they finally came to pick up their T-33s. What an honor and a privilege it was! I was an Instructor Pilot in the T-33 jet trainer beginning at Tyndall Field until I retired in July 1972.

I will return to being a T-33 jet instructor pilot later. But now, I turn to a discussion of "dragging the rag" (target) for the Army anti-aircraft folks at Colon on the Atlantic Ocean side in Panama. My flight record of towing targets in the P-51 finally caught up with me, and I was tapped to tow the target for the Army in the B-26. Why? Because the B-26 pilot and plane were assigned to our Caribbean Command to tow aerial targets for them. It was one aircraft, one pilot, and one B-26 crew chief. The pilot got into trouble with the law in Panama, and he was given orders and flown out of Panama at Tocumen Airport at 2:00 AM.

I know because, as Base Adjutant and Personnel Officer, I cut the orders. Little did I know that I would be selected to check out in the twin-engine B-26 and be ready to tow targets in two days for our Army friends! Again, no one had towed targets assigned to the Caribbean Command except your ol' P-51 pilot. I was lucky in that the friend from Guatemala was in town for two days and he had instructed in the B-26. He agreed to check me out. That B-26 only had one set of controls on the pilot's side. Chappelle showed me how to start and taxi while I sat on two coke boxes on the right side of the cockpit.

In an hour, I was flying the B-26 and had practiced *feathering* the engines (reducing propeller drag). It was a neat flying plane, but far different from a DC-3. Needless to say, I was stuck towing targets in the B-26 while we waited for a replacement from the tow target outfit in El Paso, Texas. Did I say I was *stuck* in DC-3s? Indeed I was, because I had to fly my turn as pilot in the DC-3 to Central and South America destinations. But, in between flying the DC-3 and my responsibilities as Adjutant and Personnel Officer—and yes, Protocol Officer for the Command—I was able to squeeze in several flights in the jet T-33s while still once a week supporting the Army towing targets in the B-26. Yep, I was now current as a bomber pilot, a jet fighter pilot, and cargo DC-3 pilot! In addition, I'd sometimes get a ride as co-pilot in the B-17 and C-54. This opened up lots of possibilities for a flying assignment when we left Panama for the States in 1955. I had finally worked out an assignment in F-86Ds, but it was not to be. I got my orders in May 1955, only to find out that all pilots rotating that year had to go to an ROTC assignment. My assignment was Baton Rouge, Louisiana, at LSU (Louisiana State University), a land grant college like the University of Maryland and Texas

A&M. I was heartbroken not being able to fly the combat jets; but this was even better because, if I continued in school, I could get my BS degree. Of course, I served as Detachment Adjutant, Administration and Personnel Officer, and Operations Officer. My job was to ascertain that everyone got in their required flying time and to talk ROTC cadets into becoming pilots. The Commandant of Cadets insisted that all of his officer instructors complete their degrees and/or work on Masters and or Doctorates.

The Commandant insisted that I select a Minor because I was positioned in Human Factors with only with one hundred hours to my credit. I told him I'd minor in Astronomy. He nearly died!— at least until he understood I was a certified Celestial Navigator and had used celestial navigation often in South America. My courses in Astronomy were hard courses because it had been some time since I had completed the required electives in math and astronomy as a freshman at A&M and in Air Force schools. Subsequently, I graduated from LSU in 1959 with a BS degree and a minor in Astronomy, which paid off for me later in my numerous assignments until I retired in 1972. LSU would not list either degree, but the Air University at Maxwell AFB and AFIT (Air Force Institute of Technology) couldn't have cared less. I had the hours and the BS degree, and the Air Force was happy.

Even though I was loaded to the gills in school and administering to the Air Force ROTC detachment at LSU, I still found time to fly the T-33 at Biloxi (Keesler AFB), Mississippi, and Alexandria (England AFB), Louisiana, as a T-33 Instrument Instructor. We were loaded with students at Keesler who needed checkouts and currency checks, and nearly the same at England AFB with fighter pilots (F-100s). When Keesler lost their T-33s, I moved to England AFB and didn't miss a beat in flying. When the T-33s were out for their maintenance inspections, I flew the C-123 troop carrier and the Army's *Beaver* spotter-plane—tail-dragger with a T-6 engine. I had instructed in the T-6 in earlier years.

Then we were assigned an L-17 *Navion*, a four-place single-engine Army observation plane with retractable gear and flaps. This plane was to be used for orientation rides for sophomore cadets. I was Operations and Flight Officer, so I got the job. I was responsible for the Air Science II instructors who all had to be pilots and be certified to give orientation rides. The first L-17 was underpowered and could barely carry two cadets. We were issued another, and I had to go get it in mid-winter (15 degrees) in Syracuse, New York, where it was literally buried in nearly six feet of snow.

I flew in on Mohawk Airlines from Baltimore, Maryland. When I saw the L-17, it was covered with more than five feet of snow with only the tip of one prop blade visible. How was I going to get it out of the snow and flying? Fortunately, I had a friend teaching ROTC at the University in Syracuse. His students let out for "drill," cleared off the snow, and then pulled the aircraft across the ice some fifty yards to the only hanger on base. They were kind enough to thaw out the airplane, unlock the brakes, and get the engine running. In spite of it all, the little airplane made it back to Baton Rouge and LSU.

The other three ROTC instructors and I gave orientation rides until we were blue in the face. We were able to talk several ROTC cadets into going to Air Force pilot training. It was a great experience to later run into one of them in the Air Force.

All the time I was giving rides in the L-17 and instructing sophomore ROTC cadets at LSU, I was flying T-33s as an

Instrument Instructor at Keesler (for one year) and England AFB (for two years). One Friday, after lunch, I was in class teaching, and I received an emergency call from England AFB—mind you, it was after 2:00 PM. The pilot who was calling insisted on talking only to me.

I left the class, answered the phone, and it was a Black captain I knew who was home on emergency from Aviano, Italy. He was a combat Air Force F-100 pilot. He was stuck at England AFB because they would not issue his orders to return to Aviano until he went to instrument school, flew ten hours of instruments, and passed an instrument flight check. He had taken the instrument written exam and had passed it, but there were no instrument flight instructors at England AFB. Chappie James and I were both Captains and on the Air Force list to be promoted to Major any day. We had discussed it over a beer before he left for Italy.

Chappie later became a four-star general and Commander of the US Air Defense Forces at Colorado Springs. The first thing he said to me when I got on the phone was: "Get your fanny down here right away! I've got a T-33 assigned, serviced, and ready for us to fly to get my needed ten hours, however long it takes." I tried to explain to him that I was in uniform and in class. He broke in and repeated: "Get your butt in your car and get up here! I'll be ready to takeoff in two hours." I replied back, "It takes two and a half hours just to drive!"

Anyway, I grabbed my jet helmet, flight suit, and necessary maps/charts/etc. and headed for Alexandria—my wife smiled as I whipped through the house gathering the helmet/suit, change of clothes, and over-night kit. In three hours I was at Base Operations at England AFB—fortunately without a speeding ticket!—and there stood Chappie, flight clearance in hand, ready to go. We flew night and day, stopping only for gas, food, and some needed rest Saturday night. On Sunday night, we were back at England AFB with ten hours of hard instruments under our belts. Damn it, Chappie James could fly instruments!—saved me lots of worry. We reported to Colonel Carl Taylor, Operations Officer for England AFB. He ordered me to give him an instrument check. Rules were that the ten-hour instructor could not also give the check. When I mentioned the regulation, Colonel Taylor thundered, "Who do you think made those rules?" I told him that he did. "OK," he said, "the rule is, Oliver, go give him a check and I mean a complete one!" Three hours later, by noon, we were back. Chappie passed easily.

We reported to Colonel Carl Taylor. Chappie asked him for a sign-off, "Where are my orders?" Colonel Taylor looked him square in the eye and roared: "No orders until you go through the altitude chamber ... and you too Oliver! You haven't been through in five years! I called Foster Field in Victoria, Texas. Run over there this evening. You're scheduled for the altitude chamber early tomorrow."

We took off in the same old T-33 and were in the altitude chamber at 8:00 AM the next day. That evening we were back at England AFB, and Colonel Taylor met us at the plane with all of Chappie James' papers. He was off to Aviano. All was well.

Afterwards, I didn't see Colonel Taylor for years until he called me one day from Salado, Texas. He had retired and lived in Mill Creek. I didn't see Chappie James until he was the Commanding General at the Air Defense Command in Colorado Springs. I was there visiting Air Force Space Command and went by to see him. I pulled a "Chappie James" on him and I walked right into that four-star general's office. He got the guard off my back and gave me a tour.

Jack and Miriam

(10)

SATELLITES— DISCOVERER (CORONA)

When I received my degree and left LSU (Louisiana State University) in 1958, it was a different world, but I wasn't soon to realize it. The Air Force, in their infinite wisdom, had sent me to Kessler AFB to go through the year-long Ground Electronics Officers Course. It was tough! Even though I had minored in Astronomy at LSU with its high-powered math, I was not prepared for the in-depth math I had to go through. Did I mention it was tough!—and this after over three years of college at LSU.

I didn't know that I was being prepared for a job in the Air Force fledging Discoverer (Corona) Space Program under the CIA. It was their program, and we had to be trained to be up to par with all of those well-qualified civilian contractor personnel now manning the station. Some twenty-one of us were hand-picked to end up, after training, at the Satellite Tracking Station at Vandenberg AFB. More than half were young West Point and Annapolis graduates who had just finished their Masters Degrees in Electrical Engineering. The rest were old heads in communications and electronics—I'd say one-half dozen Captains and two Chief Warrants in radar tracking; and two Majors to train in all facets of the Satellite Operations and take over in a year as Station Operations Officers. I was also to continue flying the T-33 and fly for satellite antenna bore sighting.

Most of us did not know anything about Vandenberg AFB, California, or for that matter, the old Army's Camp Cooke of WWII days. The Western Test Range had been established at Vandenberg, taking over the old infantry base. Everything was so highly-classified that a Top Secret clearance didn't even get you into the base. It took a *need-to-know* for a particular program plus that Top Secret clearance just to say "hello."

Vandenberg AFB (old Camp Cooke) was the new site for checking out missiles and launching them to the South Pacific. These were primarily Atlas and Titan Missiles, then in a few years the solid rocket Minutemen 1, 2 and 3, plus the Titan IIID for larger payloads.

When we first got to Vandenberg, there were only limited family quarters, so most of us went to nearby Santa Maria or Lompoc. We rented a house in Santa Maria from the City Mayor and drove ten miles to the Satellite Tracking Station, situated on a mountain ten miles from Santa Maria and five miles east of Vandenberg. We were remote for good reason. Our programs were not only Top Secret and need-to-know, but also restricted to certain need-to-know personnel.

When we arrived at the gate to the Satellite Tracking Station, we were not allowed in, but sent down to Vandenberg to our Test Wing Headquarters to obtain clearances and passes for the Tracking Station. Each of our individual past histories were checked thoroughly, and we were interviewed—in-detail—concerning everything we did until the time we reported to the Test Wing. These people were dead-serious about who had knowledge of and access to their programs. Sometime the next day, we were issued passes and parking space tickets for our cars at the Tracking Station plus a Vandenberg base sticker. It was a long time—months in fact—before our wives got passes into the Tracking Station. They were never permitted to visit our offices, only the lobby welcoming room.

Once we were all properly documented, we were given a tour of Vandenberg, our squadron and orderly room, and the Missile Launch Complex for the Atlas, Titan and Thor Missiles. It was a consolidated tour—yes, all in one bus to visit the Tracking Station, up on the hill, off the road to Santa Maria.

We were treated nearly as zombies at the Tracking Station. All but four people belonged to two contractor groups: LMSC (Lockheed Missiles and Space Company) and WDL (Western Development Laboratories), which became Philco-Ford in 1966.

The four included our new squadron commander, his executive officer, an R&D Officer—assigned by Systems Command—and a new R&D Officer, Harold Brashears. R&D stood for Research and Development and it covered a multitude of sins—primarily, that they always had the last word!

We didn't know it then, but we should have guessed. We were to be trained by the contractors, and after a year, take over their jobs. We were to "blue-suit" the station with Air Force personnel. It seemed that the contractors already knew the situation, or were soon to know, as they began our training. But first we were to go to our headquarters at Moffett Field, near San Francisco, to be briefed on our mission and set our training schedules. Then our group was broken down. All those in operations were moved across the street to WDL/Philco to train as Satellite Master Controllers, while others were trained by WDL and LMSC to maintain and run the station.

We had no trouble with WDL/Philco. They had a history from day one with the Air Force in installing com-electronic equipment all over the world, running and operating the equipment, and then moving on.

I began my training as a Satellite Master Controller in early 1960 with WDL/Philco. They trained me well, and I worked the consoles twelve-on, twelve-off for six months until they felt I could handle the next job as Satellite Operations Officer. This was not easy because we had a contract with Lockheed LMSC to manage the Satellite Tracking Station. It was quite obvious that they knew we were training to take their management jobs, and they were training us to do so. Fortunately for us, there were good LMSC personnel. They were well-trained and managed, understood what was going on, and appreciated the importance of the Tracking Stations to work with the Agena Satellite that LMSC had developed with the help of Clarence "Kelly" Johnson in the Lockheed *Skunk Works*. It had been planned to mate the Agena with the Atlas Missile in a couple of years, but we needed most of our Atlas Missiles in the missile race. The Air Force believed the Russians had a multitude of international missiles, and we had only a few in testing. So the Air Force used Thor Missiles, returned from England and Turkey, for the Agena.

President Eisenhower was deeply concerned. We tried to photograph any existing Russian missile sites with the high-flying U-2 and some four hundred balloons with cameras floating over Russia. Less than a dozen balloons actually covered the proper areas and provided few usable photographs. President Eisenhower ordered the Agena Satellite development in 1958 and the positioning of a matrix of tracking stations around the world for polar launching and tracking Agena Satellites.

The program was so highly-classified that only a few people in the Air Force knew about it, still fewer in contractor circles. Lockheed managers, and even Air Force supervisors, were not told of its intended use. Since Russia had launched *Sputnik* and was pushing future manned space flight, the United States played on that theme. We were tasked to strongly project that we had sent up monkeys and conducted other related tests to ensure the notion that we had "men in space."

The program was known as *Discoverer* to all the people on the project from top-down to the last Air Force person or contractor at the Launch Complex or Tracking Stations. The Air Force was to be the operational manager in partnership with the CIA (Central Intelligence Agency), who owned the project.

In all the time I was in training as a Satellite Master Controller and Satellite Operations Officer over the Satellite Master Controllers, I never once knew or was informed that I was working for the CIA. After over a year, I was assigned as one of two Satellite Operations Officers—twelve-on, twelve-off—as manager of the operational activities of the Tracking Station. A few weeks later, we took over the CIA's role at the station. We were briefed to never disclose the CIA's participation, the *Corona* name, or to even mention the CIA—never! This continued even when I left Vandenberg and took command of the Kaena Point Tracking Station in Hawaii, assigned temporary duty to JTF-8 and the Pacific atomic tests, B-29 air drops, and Thor/Atomic Bomb launches at Johnston Island—where I was Project Coordinator, even as a Major. I then went to SAMSO (Space and Missiles and Satellite Operations) Headquarters at El Segundo, Los Angeles, California, as Chief of Staff for Plans and Operations. There I was alerted that I was the CIA contact tasked with reviewing any personnel clearances and monitoring operations. Later I went to the Defense Communications Agency (DCA) in Washington, DC, with duty station at Fort Monmouth, New Jersey. My boss was my old CIA supervisor in Los Angeles and now at Fort Monmouth. Upon retiring, I asked him when I would be debriefed. He looked me squarely in the eyes and cautioned, "Never! And don't try anything funny." I haven't.

A lot of activity had taken place at Vandenberg AFB since the contract was issued to LMSC to manage the program and continue developing and improving the Agena Satellite. For a decade, our CIA Corona Satellite Cold War Program was treated as if it didn't exist. A dozen missions failed before one in 1960 (Discoverer XIV) succeeded in delivering intelligence imagery back from outer space. A dozen more failures occurred through 1961. I was in training when we launched those early vehicles. But as I became qualified to count down a vehicle for launch in 1961, it became very personal to me to watch failure after failure. It was hard for me to remember that this was a totally new program fighting for entry into space—a first-ever endeavor. The first successful mission in August 1960—our fourteenth mission—covered more than 1.6 million square miles of Soviet territory, far more than the 214 flights of the U-2 over four years. President Eisenhower was elated. The intelligence gap filled quickly. In September 1961, after five successful Corona Missions, the CIA cut sharply its estimate of Russia's long range missiles. We had believed them to have completed 140 to 200 launchers, when there could only have been between 10 to 25 using our best interpretations of photographs from our Corona missions.

After our 11th Corona (Discoverer) Mission failure, President Eisenhower called the Director of the National Reconnaissance Office (NRO) and the Director of the CIA into his office—the Oval Office. He quickly got to the point. Failures had to stop! The United States needed good intelligence and needed it now! Years later in Colorado Springs, when the NRO Director debriefed us on the Corona program—we were then cleared to talk about it—he related that story of General Eisenhower calling him and the CIA Director into his office: "After giving us a dressing-down, he went behind his desk, pulled down the US flag and pole, and laid them across his desk. He unfastened the flag, folded it up—more like wadded it up—and forcefully shoved it into my gut and said, 'Take this US Flag and put it into the nose cone of our next Thor-Agena launch. And I want you two to bring it back to me in seventeen days, after the flight and recovery.' He then added, 'There had better not be a tear, rip, or burn on its surface!' How were we to guarantee a success after all those failures? But it was a perfect countdown, beautiful launch, and a perfect flight and recovery!"

The NRO and CIA Directors took the flag back to President Eisenhower, as ordered. The President laid it out once again on his desk. It was in good shape—no tear, rip, or burn. The President looked at them and exclaimed, "Now see, it can be done!" and added, "Now give me a successful flight with lots of intelligence!" He wanted pictures!

I was involved with that countdown as a Satellite Master Controller trainee. We spent hours and days working electronically with the Agena satellite sitting on top of the Thor which was miles away on the launch pad. After numerous checks, everything appeared fine. The launch was perfect, and it went into orbit as planned. The satellite made seventeen orbits of the earth and filmed 1.6 million miles of Russian territory, from submarines and ships in the north, to military installations all over Russia, to the missile pads and new construction in the south and southeast. The Agena was reoriented for re-entry, retro rockets fired, and the nose cone—loaded with intelligence film—returned to earth and snatched in mid-air by one of our C-119 aircraft southwest of Hawaii.

Over a period of twelve years—from August 1960 to the last Corona Satellite mission recovery on May 31, 1972—145 Corona flights returned 165 capsules from space containing 866,000 frames of film covering the nearly 100 million square miles of the USSR plus six million square miles of the United States. The Discoverer 13 Capsule is on display in the Smithsonian, and the Discoverer 14 Capsule is in the Air Force Museum near Dulles Airport in Washington, DC. I was privileged to take part in the preparation and launch of both capsules and their tracking while in orbit. I was also able to listen to the live audio of the retrieval in the Pacific Ocean by our recovery forces. I have a piece of the first parachute from space, mounted as a Special Award given to me in 1967 by the Satellite Recovery people. I had just completed four years as Commander of the Satellite Tracking Station at Kaena Point, Hawaii, where we had tracked the satellites in their space orbits and helped the recovery aircraft pinpoint the return locations for intercept.

Hawaii had been good to me. I pinned on my Lieutenant Colonel insignia on arrival to Kaena Point in 1964, and shortly thereafter was made Commander of the station. It was a great and fulfilling four years. Our Corona program was in its prime, as were several additional developing satellite programs, and we did our best in support of NASA and their Kauai Station. I continued to fly with the Hawaiian National Guard for the four years in their T-33 trainers as an instrument instructor and served as a "target" plane for their fighter interceptors. Seldom did they miss finding me, whether it was night or day, over water, at altitude, or in bad weather. They were good!

We loved the people and climate in Hawaii, as well as Pearl Harbor, Hickam and Wheeler Air Force Bases, and all their associated history. We visited all of the bases and Tripler Army Medical Center regularly. We were active in several community organizations. It was difficult to think about leaving our many military and civilian friends when we ultimately received our orders to leave. And the same was true for our boys who were active in school functions and loved to surf on Oahu shores. They were good at it!

But when the boys found out we were to go back to California on a ship, they became enthused. We were fortunate to get two cabins on the steamship SS *Lurline* on its last trip to the mainland. We all made the most of it. What a way to leave Hawaii—with such an "Aloha," streamers trailing to the dock, and the singing of Auld Lang Syne!

There was no way I can break from the Corona Satellite narrative without relating the story of AFSC (Air Force Systems Command) loaning me to the AEC's JTF-8 (Joint Task Force) to go to the South Pacific in 1962. Our satellites were not directly used in the JTF-8 tests, only the Thor booster to lift the atomic bombs. I was lead controller at Vandenberg AFB for the MIDAS (Missile Detection and Surveillance) Satellite program which was highly classified. After putting the MIDAS program to bed for several weeks, with only data readouts, I was loaned to AEC (JTF-8) for six months. I truly believe I owe a tribute to my fellow JTF-8 folks and other atomic exercise volunteers over the years who in the end gave their lives participating in the tests. Of the two hundred men at Johnston Island, including the Commanding General, I only know of a few survivors—I, of course, being one.

THE ATOMIC TESTS

In the middle of winter, 1961–62, after successfully completing one of our first MIDAS Satellite flights—an Agena with MIDAS payload, atop an Atlas Missile—I was primary Satellite Operations Officer on the MIDAS Satellite as was George Scuffos on the SAMOS Satellite. The SAMOS payload was also mated to the Atlas Missile for launch and was an ongoing program. Both Scuffos and I were still expected to act as Satellite Master Controllers on our twelve-hour shifts as active controllers for the Corona (Discoverer) Satellite Program.

Upon the successful launch of the MIDAS Satellite and a highly successful mission with great readout returns from space, I was asked by General "Red" Moore, our Commanding General, to come to Sunnyvale to receive a Commendation for the Vandenberg Tracking Station, and to be personally presented, by the General, the Air Force Commendation Medal. This was quite an honor to be so recognized.

When I returned to Vandenberg from reporting to General Moore, I was met at the door by our Commanding Officer with orders for me to report to the Pentagon at 8:00 AM the following Monday for further instructions. I had a feeling that our commander was hoping to get rid of me. Needless to say, I reported as directed. After receiving clearances and verification for AEC (Atomic Energy Commission), I was briefed on my assignment.

I was to be assigned as the Frequency Controller and Projects Coordinator for the JTF-8 projects on Johnston Island, Christmas Island, and the North and South Conjugate areas (near the Samoan Islands). The *USS Hornet* Aircraft Carrier was to serve as the Command Post for the B-29 atomic bomb air drops. After a full briefing, the Commanding General of JTF-8, General Starbird, send me to Hawaii as his advance party before the test. It was my job to get HQ PACAF (Pacific Air Forces Headquarters) and their four military departments on-board with the projects. I have never seen such cooperation and support!

I had an office on the *USS Hornet*, our Command Post, but I was required to be with the British on Christmas Island most of the time. It seemed that it was the Brits' job to teach me to drink and hold Beefeater Gin—two-plus shots to a previous single one! I had been formerly indoctrinated with early space contractors and program folks, so I managed to survive. I still like Beefeaters!

After the B-29 airdrops of atomic bombs, we moved to Johnston Island, 860 miles west-southwest (WSW) of the Hawaiian Islands. My office was now on the *USNS Range Tracker*, an instrumentation ship from Point Magu just south of Vandenberg AFB. My jobs were the same—Frequency Interference Coordinator and

Projects Manager. Our launch complex was on the south end of the island and included a Thor Missile launch complex—like we had at Vandenberg a few miles north of Point Magu. There was also a holding stash for the atomic bombs to be lunched atop the Thor Missile.

We had several dry runs on Johnston Island—a one square-mile sand and coral island in the Pacific. Only the Launch Controller was on the *USNS Range Tracker*, while General Starbird hung out in the bunker. Unfortunately, the Navy failed to provide a seasoned, qualified Launch Controller, which was to later cause us troubles. Initially, we conducted a couple of successful launches and atomic bomb bursts over Johnston Island—atomic bombs were typically detonated at five to one hundred miles up. Then a twenty-five kiloton (25,000 tons of TNT) atomic bomb was mated to the Thor booster and subsequently launched. At fifteen hundred feet, the missile drifted off course a few degrees and the Launch Controller immediately destroyed the atomic bomb and missile just above the Island! We never quite understood the reason for this because there was open water on every side!

Pieces of the missile and atomic bomb obviously fell back on Johnston Island. Everyone was safely in the bunker except for the launch control folks and a few of us on the *USNS Range Tracker*. Several falling fragments from the highly toxic atomic bomb just missed us! Debris was scattered all over the island.

After several minutes, I got a call from General Starbird in the Bunker. He told me to get my Frequency Control Team together and clear a path to the mess hall for him and his staff. I cautioned him that it was pretty dangerous with those fragments of uranium from the atomic bomb strewn everywhere. But he quickly reminded me that it was my duty to locate the debris from the atomic bomb, mark and stack them, and clear a path to the mess hall. This we did, as quickly as we could. Soon we escorted the General and his staff to the Holmes and Narver Mess Hall. We spent days cleaning up the debris, working with specialists from Pearl Harbor.

I do not know of any of the bunker participants, including the General, who later survived the ordeal—all reportedly died of some form of radiation sickness. I do know that a couple of days later, we launched our next atomic bomb off of the island. Fortunately, we had no more launch problems after the one that was destroyed.

As indicated earlier, I was on loan to JTF-8 as a Frequency Expert and telemetry person. When the launches ended, I was sent back to my tracking station at Vandenberg AFB in California. Of course, there were no records or notices of exposure to numerous air-launched B-29 bombs and their radiation. Nor were there any exposure records of the many Thor Missiles ground-launched from Johnston Island and their accompanying radiation. As the bombs burst, we could count and see the bones in our fingers, just like x-rays. We wore no exposure meters, so no one really knew what effects it had. We just received a pat on the back and were sent back home to our parent outfits. As time went by, we slowly got reports of the passing of the JTF-8 participants beginning with General Starbird, my big boss, Colonel Ellis Mist, my immediate boss, and Colonel Mike Meyer, the Launch Director. I know of only three folks on Johnston Island who survived (and I count our blessing)—a friend, John Caldwell, an Australian, and yours truly.

*(L) Thor-Agena A in the National Museum
of the USAF (USAF photo)
(R) Atlas-Agena A 45D (MIDAS) Air Force
Space and Missile Museum*

Jack was responsible, directly or indirectly, for many of the 145 launches, tracking, readout and recovery of the Thor/Agena-Corona Satellites (1960–69). He was also primary officer on the Atlas/Agena-MIDAS Satellite and backup for the first Atlas/Agena-SAMOS Satellites. His responsibilities continued at Johnston Island in 1962 with the JTF-8 tests as Projects Coordinator for the Thor missile launches with assorted atomic warheads. The Agena Space Vehicle was used in large numbers during the 1960s and 1970s as upper stage with SLV-2 Thor, SLV-3 Atlas, and SLV-5 Titan boosters to launch a variety of military and civilian payloads into orbit.

SPACE AND MISSILES (SAMSO)

When I was loaned to the atomic JTF-8 tests in 1962 from the Vandenberg Tracking Station, one of my contacts in Hawaii was Lt Col Don Werbeck, Deputy Commander of the Satellite Recovery Group. He was most helpful in my activities as the advance party to Hawaii for JTF-8. While I was getting acquainted at the Recovery Group Headquarters and Kaena Point two years later in 1964, he again proved to be a good friend. He was soon promoted to full Colonel and assigned to SAMSO (Space and Missiles and Satellite Operations) Headquarters in Los Angeles. He said he would see us again. He soon took over as Chief of Staff, Plans and Operations, for SAMSO, which administered and planned all US Missiles and Satellites and both the East and Western Test Ranges. My reassignment orders had me going to Los Angeles to SAMSO in the summer of 1967 to report to Colonel Donald Werbeck as his Deputy. I quickly learned that he worked from daylight to o-dark-thirty and he expected you to be right there with him. He had me check out in the *Blue Canoe*, a four-place twin engine Cessna 310 to carry the Deputy Commander from Los Angeles International to San Bernardino for weekly Minuteman Missile briefings. These were on Tuesday and Thursday of each week and were called *Blue Tuesday* and *Gray Thursday*. Oh yes, there was also a *Black Saturday*! I was given a weekend to check out in the Cessna 310 and had to drop anything I was doing to fly and escort the Deputy Commander on those Blue and Gray days.

There is no way I could play down the importance of those Minutemen I, II, and III briefings on Tuesdays and Thursdays and the Command's *Black Saturday* briefing on the weekends covering all SAMSO programs, the test ranges, and projects. The Corona Satellite Program, at first, did not show that the United States was far behind Russia. This all changed! We soon found we were indeed behind! We needed those Minutemen Missiles to fill the gap. Ten-to-one without! The Minuteman I was already outdated, and we were having trouble with the solid propellants on Minutemen II and III. The Atlas Missiles and Titans were not keeping up with Russian developments. And here I was new on the job. I had no time to really break into the job when Colonel Werbeck was suddenly transferred to Washington, DC, and promoted to Brigadier General. I was moved into his position overnight and promoted to full Colonel. But then was I surprised a few days later when I came to work and a strange man was in my chair at *my* desk! He welcomed me and told me he was Edward Teller—Chairman of the President's Committee on Space, Missiles, and Nuclear Weapons—and that he would be using my desk, my office, and even my secretary for a few days. The next day I was met by another gentleman, sporting a German accent—on that same committee—Werner Von Braun, who took over my new temporary desk. I was without a desk!

What an honor and a privilege it was to have the father of our atomic bomb program, Ed Teller, and the father of our missile and space programs, Werner Von Braun, using my office and my desks—both of them! More importantly, General Werbeck's previous secretary—now mine, or at least soon-to-be-mine again— knew everything, including where the skeletons were all hidden. Our guests quickly realized how key she was to it all. She possessed a host of clearances to every program, including those from the Atomic Energy Commission, and nearly anything you could touch in our Missile and Space Programs. Two other committee members were Dr. Hans Mark, who served as NASA's Director and Chancellor for the University of Texas, and Mr. Packard of the Packard Bell Corporation. And there were others. They kept working, did their thing, and ignored the fact that I was nearby trying to get on board my new job as Chief of Staff, Plans and Operations, for our SAMSO Command. Dr. Teller and Werner Von Braun came by often and borrowed our facility, but we seldom saw the other dozen or so members unless a committee meeting was called. Then I got lost.

Colonel Werbeck—now Brig Gen Don Werbeck—was the Chief of Staff for Systems Command under four-star General Bernard Schriever, who was our military leader (from the start) for all of our missiles and satellites. He made good use of our atomic stockpile of weapons.

I kept pinching myself to see if it were really true, that this little country boy from Belton, Texas, was actually a full Colonel in this position of such great responsibility, working with and sharing knowledge with some of the greatest minds in the world. My wife and I had adopted our Commanding General, Bernard Schriever—or perhaps he adopted us—several years ago when I was commanding the Satellite Tracking Station at Kaena Point, Hawaii. The General liked to come to Hawaii several times a year just to get away and to play a little golf on the island of Maui. He was an "old" graduate of Texas A&M, and I was a Texas Aggie too. He paid no attention to the fact that my Astronomy Degree was from LSU (Louisiana State University). To him, I was a Texas Aggie, and it was my job to meet him, his crew, and any accompanying staff. It seemed that there was always one or two of them with him. Even when his IG (Inspector General) Team or any other member of his staff came to Hawaii, we were alerted and expected to meet them and see that they were taken care of. My wife, Miriam, always invited and entertained them at our home with great Hawaiian food and the best Mai Tais, a neat Hawaiian rum drink of the islands. We were their home away from home. It was difficult for our new Recovery Group Commander to assume those "duties." After we had welcomed Gen Schriever and his wife for so long, they didn't want to allow anyone else to take over. They liked being pampered by Miriam Oliver!

I enjoyed every day of my assignment to SAMSO, Space and Missiles and Satellite Operations, in spite of the constant, ever-changing pressure of the job. And despite the unusual traffic patterns and flight procedures required to fly out of LAX to San Bernardino with our Deputy Commander for the Minuteman briefings, all went well. But all good things must come to an end. I was interviewed for and briefed for a job with the DCA (Defense Communications Agency) in Washington, DC, with a duty station at Fort Monmouth, New Jersey. DCA was given responsibility for a new Defense Satellite Communications System, DSCS II. The DSCS II satellites were being designed, built, and tested by

TRW, a SAMSO contractor. Obviously, I knew about the program in detail and had visited the factory several times.

What I didn't know was that the Army had been given responsibility to build the large new satellite dishes to work with the DCA's DSCS II wideband communication satellites. We had thought that one of SAMSO's old contractors in northern California would get the job. It didn't happen. The Army's Contract Management got the job to contract for the huge antennas. A very old West Pointer—an old, old Air Force Colonel—was supposed to be monitoring the Army's activities at Fort Monmouth. He was doing nothing. He had been in the Army Contract Management three-star general's class at West Point. He was giving the Army General a fit, and the General wanted him to go. The old Air Force Colonel in question insisted that he be given "general's quarters" at Fort Monmouth, New Jersey, and also be provided a full-time staff car. He had everyone upset, including the General, and they wanted DCA in Washington, DC, to replace him without delay.

I requested permission to go to Fort Monmouth and get the lay of the land from the Army's Communications Satellite Agency Organization (ACSA) that we routinely worked with on all sorts of evolving communications projects. I also made an appointment with the old Colonel through Code 400 at DCA for a definite date and time. Upon arrival, I found he had gone to Washington, DC, to expedite his retirement and he did not care to see me. I visited with the Army Communications Satellite folks and the old colonel's wife. She showed me their quarters and was nice, but she knew nothing except that they would be leaving soon. However, the Communications Satellite people were *not* so nice. They had no use for the Colonel and told me so. He had never tried to help them from the day he reported in. It looked like I was in for a long, cold period.

I went back to Los Angeles, stopping by Washington, DC, and Code 400, DCA, to see my new boss. He was a neat guy, a new Brigadier General, Lewis Norman, and he expected me to do great things, having worked with him in Los Angeles. You will notice that I sometimes eliminate names. Having been under the CIA and cognizant of such, I was very careful about who did what to whom? Most often my cautiousness worked out in the long run.

When I returned to Los Angeles, it was suddenly obvious that I had been picked to clean up the problem with the Army. Three contacts later—with SAMSO Headquarters, Air Force Systems Command, and the Air Force—they cut the orders sending me to Code 400, Washington, DC, as Chief of the East Coast Field Office, with duty station at Fort Monmouth, New Jersey, Defense Communications Agency (DCA). The Communications Satellite Agency had a great history. They had three Civil Service PL-313s assigned. Those three had planned and launched the first US satellite from Wallops Island in 1958. I felt a kindred spirit with these early US Missilers, as they had with me in the Corona Program. Without them, my assignment to the DCA Field Office and my work with the Army's Communications Satellite Agency would have failed. Also, I had a secretary with every clearance in the world, and she was Top Secret Control Officer for special projects at Fort Monmouth—our program too! Gladys Fabino was a princess, a dear one, who came along at the right time. And she had survived the old, old Air Force colonel. On my second day at Fort Monmouth, I decided to meet the three PL-313s, all equal to "star" generals.

I was pleasantly surprised. They were all familiar with our Corona Satellite Program in the 1960s, and I was expected to know all about their launch of our first satellite into space from Wallops Island in response to Russia's *Sputnik*. They knew Ed Teller, Werner Von Braun, and my other SAMSO contacts. And, they adopted me! On my second day at the Communications Satellite Agency, I asked to meet the Commander. At 10:00 AM sharp, I reported. From the Commanders desk, turned backwards, came: "Hello, Jack Oliver. Welcome aboard! This is George Rippey from Hawaii, the one you took the newly-developed and most confidential antenna away from!" I thought I was in trouble, but not true. As mentioned, Colonel Rippey was Chief of Communications and Electronics for the 25th Infantry Division before Vietnam. The third PL-313 was his man. Now I had all three PL-313s on my side and also the unit's Commander. There was hope!

At the end of my first month, there was a Command golf tournament. We were expected to take part. I was so bad in golf that we were positioned as the last foursome with George Brown, one of those 313s at the Communications Satellite Agency. He arranged for me to meet everyone, including the three-star commanding general. He laid it out to me. I assured him it was a new world.

From that day forward, the DCA Field Office at Fort Monmouth was there to work with and support every communications program, and in particular our DSCS II Satellite Terminal Program. It was several weeks before I was accepted by the Communications Satellite Agency's staff. That old Air Force Colonel had left a bad taste in everyone's mouth. I did have one leg up, not two, because I had two of the three PL-313s on my side plus the Commander of the Communications Satellite Agency, Colonel George Rippey. I had worked closely with him regarding communications and required electronics associated with the projects on Johnston Island, the South Conjugate (Samoan Islands) sites, and those in the Alaskan chain of islands. He and his office were most helpful throughout the atomic tests.

Colonel Rippey's Contract Management Division was now responsible for not only the contract for a dozen 60-foot wideband satellite dishes (terminals) for our DSCS II Satellites, but he was also prime contractor for ten other communications programs, from Auto-Von, to Auto-SeVo Com, to every conceivable classified and routine communication system used, or in-planning, by all of the services—Air Force, Army, Navy, and Marines.

Well, Philco-Ford—later Ford-Neutronics of Palo Alto and Sunnyvale, California—was awarded the contract for designing and building the new 60-foot dishes. The company's project engineer, soon to be on station at Fort Monmouth, was an old friend who had trained me as a Satellite Master Controller at Vandenberg in 1960. We were, and continue to be, close friends. Needless to say, I had no trouble, ever, with the contractor from day one. Cliff Ray understood both sides of the equation because, from the start, he had been with satellites and the development of the large 60-foot antennas used in our Corona, SAMOS, MIDAS and other key satellite programs.

We made a great team. His contractor folks thought I belonged to them, and I felt they belonged to me. There were no secrets between any of us. Nor were there secrets with the Communications Satellite Agency's key folks, especially those PL-313s. In fact we finally got one of the PL-313s to move to

Washington, DC, and take up office in Code 400, DCA. This worked out well. When we finished the program and accepted our first operational 60-foot terminals, I was ready to retire with thirty years of service. I wrote a staff study to the Commanding General, DCA, and my Code 400 boss and recommended we do away with my office. The Communications Satellite Agency was working so well with DCA that no oversight office was needed. And the PL-313 from the Communications Satellite Agency worked so efficiently with DCA in Washington, DC, that they just left him there.

It was time for me to go home to Texas. Because my staff study to disband my DCA Field Office at Fort Monmouth was approved, I promptly submitted my request for my thirty-year retirement as of July 1, 1972. My request was accepted, and I was retired with great fanfare by the Army and our DCA Code 400 staff at Fort Monmouth, New Jersey. What a great assignment from 1969 to July 1972! My DCA supervisors had found out that activities at Fort Monmouth were working out so well, that my Code 400 supervisor—my old CIA boss at SAMSO—had me on the road visiting the associated Army, Air Force, Navy and Marine Corps activities as they related to the satellite (DSCS II) terminals and any other communications issues. And General Lewis Norman had me visit the prime antenna contractor, WDL, all of the many subcontractors from Massachusetts to Florida, several California companies and locations, our old SAMSO, and Satellite Control in Palo Alto. It seemed I was always on a red-eye flight from the west coast on Sunday night, arriving in Washington, DC, at daybreak on Monday, and ready to give a full briefing at 9:00 AM sharp to the Commanding General and his staff. Needless to say, my many trips were not solely related to DSCS II. Test Ranges, Satellites and Missiles, and their contractors were also thrown into the pot.

What a send off! What a pat on the back for my service! Not only was I honored for my thirty years of service, but DCA presented me with the Legion of Merit for my service to them. I was overwhelmed.

We took the long way home after retirement and went to California and the West Coast by way of Las Vegas. We saw some good shows but didn't stay long because we don't gamble. It was off to California to see our two sons. One was married to a lovely girl named Rory, and the other was scheduled to marry Anna at a big "Greek wedding" upon our arrival in Los Angeles. Our son Robert was a minister at our President's old church in California. It was a great celebration. As soon as the newlyweds were off on their honeymoon, we bounced over to visit his brother in Torrance for a couple of days. Then we were off to Texas to see if we were ready for retirement.

We had purchased a GI farm with my dad in 1952 when we were in Panama. In a couple of years, we bought him out. We paid on that 208-acre farm for forty years, but it was the greatest investment I ever made. When my dad died in 1990, we sold the 208-acre farm and moved to our old home, Three Forks, where I was born and raised. Mom and dad had both been in rest homes, and we were their will/estate administrators and executors. No one wanted their old home, so we took it as our share—one quarter of the estate.

When we returned to Texas in the fall of 1972, we were home—"Full Circle." We left home in November 1942 when we entered WWII service from Texas A&M and came home in July 1972.

Colonel and Mrs. Jack Oliver
Christmas 1990

(12)

FULL CIRCLE—
COMING HOME

When I enlisted in the Air Corps in 1942, I never realized I would make it "Full Circle" and return to my old home in Three Forks, Texas. Of course, I didn't actually return to my birth place until 1994 after my mother died. We had bought a 208-acre GI farm from the State Land Board with my dad in 1952–53. A friend of ours was recalled to active duty and sold his 208-acre farm to dad and me in 1952–53. In a few years, dad sold out to me with the understanding that I would pay my kid brother Mike's way at Texas A&M College. It was a great deal for everyone and one which I enjoyed fully. My brother Mike not only received his BS degree at A&M but also obtained his Masters there soon after. We all had the best of both worlds. Mike, who was eighteen years younger than I, helped dad farm the 208 acres while he was in high school. Then before college, he helped dad run his own 192-acre farm in our old home place, Three Forks, five miles east of Belton on the Little River/Academy Road. This was where we were born and raised.

Our 208-acre GI farm had a small two-bedroom farm home on it. A couple of years before we came home to stay, we spent two summer vacations making the house livable and putting a new Tennessee Valley metal roof on it. We had community water piped in and hooked up to the house. We also had our livestock water well as a backup. We were preparing our temporary nest because our new three thousand square-foot ranch home would not be ready for three or four years. Our new home was contracted out to Johnnie Melvin, a Belton builder, my old high school classmate, on a pay-as-you-go deal. The first year, we cleared a foundation and laid a concrete slab with copper plumbing under the slab. The second year, we framed out the structure, put on the roof, and piped water to the site from the cottage, including both community and our own well water lines. The third year, in the spring before we were to retire, we had the house totally bricked, including a fireplace and chimney. We were due home in July or August of 1972.

When we arrived home in late July 1972, the house was ready for inside finish—sheetrock, cabinets, built-ins, dual hot water heaters, two septic tanks, proper insulation, and air conditioners.

The house was fully electric. We were the last Gold Medal home to be approved in our county in 1972–73, which meant reasonable electric rates and discounts on appliance purchases. We took advantage every way we could. My wife and I became certified finishers for our home because of all of the sheetrock work. I'll be crippled for life for putting those four- by eight-foot ceiling panels in place. We finally worked out a scaffolding system. We did finishing work around windows, doors, and closets. We felt that we became experts at it over time. We did contract out the kitchen and bathroom cabinets, but our original home plumber completed our three baths, kitchen, and wash room.

We had ordered all new furniture for the new house, so we left all of our old furniture, including a king-sized bed, in the abandoned cottage. We moved into our grand new ranch home in the summer of 1973. Wouldn't you think our children, their families, and our friends would want to visit us and stay in our new home? Not on your life! They insisted on staying in our cottage, on the creek, near the pond. They made it their guest house until we sold it in 1993. We then moved to Three Forks, to our old family farm house, in 1994. My mother had passed away and left the house as part of my inheritance. When we moved into mom and dad's old farm home—built in 1921 and where we three older kids were born and raised—it was "Full Circle" for me. It was reported that I was born at the foot of a rainbow.

We had enjoyed our 208-acre prairie farm for forty years, vacationing in the Darrs Creek cabin for many years, and living like kings on a hill in our new ranch home for over twenty years. Years ago we had purchased forty acres of land from mom and dad on the north side of FM 436, the ten-mile road from Belton to Little River. It was the north part of dad's 192-acre farm left to him by his Uncle Gus. Of course, he had to buy off his siblings for some of the land, but the family home was his, a marriage gift from his Uncle Gus.

My dad died at the VA hospital in Temple, Texas, Christmas 1989. Our mother had been in the rest home at Park Place Manor for six years, since it opened. We had just moved into our new home on the forty-acre tract when mom died in 1994. I had been made executor and administrator of my mom and dad's will. When he died, on the advice of our lawyer, I elected to wait for my mother's demise and settle the estate with my three siblings at that time. The remaining 150 acres in dad's farm were divided four ways, each of us getting 37½ acres. My brother Ben and sister Ann wanted to sell their acreage to their siblings at a price set by dad. No one wanted the old farm home with its expenses. I gladly took their offers. It meant everything to me. I was born there.

Mom's home was fully furnished, and we lived there for several months while they finished our new home in the north pasture across the road. My brother Mike sold me his 37½-acre inheritance plus 37½ acres sold to him by my sister Ann. That gave me the 75 acres on the south end of the 150 acres. My brother Ben asked me to take his 37½ acres at the going price. We now owned all of dad's 150 acres plus the 40 acres to the north. We thus had the entire 192-acre farm that my great uncle Ben and great Uncle Gus had purchased in 1874. My wife Miriam and I continued to farm the land and run cattle on it, just as our two far-sighted great uncles had done.

After we had completed our 208-acre prairie home on the farm out of Holland, Texas, we were asked to run for County Commissioner for Bell County for Precinct 4. After we won the election in 1979, we put a runway on the farm and bought a Piper 140, a four-place airplane. After a year, we realized we needed a better, faster plane to enable us to visit our two boys in California, Miriam's two sisters on the east coast, and efficiently cover the County Commissioner job in a timely manner. As if heaven had heard us, we got a call from our old Panama friend, E.C. Chappelle. He had a four-place Mooney lined up—just the plane for us! It had a constant speed propeller, retractable gear, plus great range and speed.

Miriam had not seen her mother in Charleston, South Carolina, in some time, so we thought, "Why not fly to Charleston in our Piper 140, visit your mom and sister, and then go on up to

Manassas, Virginia, to look over the Mooney?" We followed our plan, arrived at Manassas, took one spin around the traffic pattern, and bought the airplane! But wait a minute! We couldn't trade or sell the Piper 140, so we had to fly the P-140 back to Killeen, Texas, and try to sell it there. It was hard to leave our new Mooney sitting in Virginia, but in a couple of weeks, I caught a ride to pick it up.

This started a 25-year love affair with that four-place Mooney. It was everything my wife and I had expected. For the twelve years that I was County Commissioner, we flew the Mooney to every National County Commissioners Conference in the United States and the State of Texas. We also made many trips to see our boys in California and to see Miriam's folks on the east coast. It was a fast, reliable airplane that helped assure we would never miss a Bell County Commissioners Court meeting or any important activities pertaining to the Court. After twenty-five years in the plane, I had to sell it because I could no longer pass the FAA flight physical for my license—I was getting old. I had passed my 83rd birthday, but it was the old accident associated with the B-29 bomber in 1948 that came back to haunt me and do me in.

The only good thing that came out of that B-29 accident was that I had been given fifty percent disability by the VA for that misfortune. Since I had been often exposed to radiation from the Atomic Bomb blasts at Christmas and Johnston Island, and the VA agreed to determine if I "glowed" every year, I have stayed with the VA. Years ago they reviewed my disability and raised it to sixty percent. Four years ago, they reviewed it again for combat related injuries. Because I was checking out in the B-29 to go to the Pacific to fly in the Korean War, Combat-Related Special Compensation (CRSC) was not approved, but my VA rating was made permanent. I concur with the VA's rating of one hundred percent because each day I am becoming more and more disabled. I now use a cane and have a walker to help on longer walks. The specialists say my fractured spine caused in the B-29 accident is now triggering lots of problems with my tendons and nerves. I am no longer upset with the FAA examiner for failing to renew my medical license to fly that great Mooney.

Even worse now is that I'm not allowed on my big John Deere farm tractor to do work around the farm. I love a clean pasture, and I did shred and mow a lot of it myself.

Tractors are a big thing for farmers and a necessity. When I came home in 1972, a friend and our butane dealer sold us his Ford 9N tractor. It was a pistol and would easily drive you through any fence if you didn't watch it while you were shredding. A friend of ours, Retired Sergeant John Churchill, introduced us to a slip clutch on the power takeoff. Our fence posts were saved! Dad sold us his big Ford 950, with twice the horsepower of the Ford 9N. We sold the Ford 9N to some unsuspecting sole. A couple of years later, we bought our first diesel tractor. It was great but needed more horsepower. We sold the Ford 950 to Mr. Huey in south Belton and traded the new diesel for a fifty-horsepower IH (International Harvester) diesel. We have had the IH 574 for nearly thirty years. It is great! Using a box blade, it has allowed us to keep all of our roads up, and it hauls nearly all of our big, round bales into storage—or out—to feed our cows (now heifers).

In 2008, I decided to buy a new 65-horsepower John Deere tractor with front-end loader and a new shredder (mower). We can haul, in or out, two big round bales to feed our heifers. It can cover lots of ground to shred the fields and pastures. We also kept the IH 574 for John to use. He keeps our pastures looking like mowed lawns and our fence rows and roads picture-perfect. I have now been ordered by my primary surgeon to keep off of the tractors—no more shredding or hauling, even on my new John Deere. I can remember our old 1938 WC Allis Chalmers 29-HP tractor—with lugs on the rear wheels—that I used to farm dad's 192 acres while he was off in the military. I even had two mules and a wagon for cotton.

In addition to tractors, a farmer-stockman requires a good pickup and trailers for many uses. I went through a series of Toyota *Tacoma* small four-wheel drive pickups over a thirty-year period. It was great for running the roads when I was County Commissioner. I also had a four-wheel drive three-quarter-ton Chevrolet for heavy duty and bad weather operation. I still have the four-by-four Chevy but traded the *Tacoma* for a *Corolla* four-door car. It's easy to get into and fall out of, even on the farm. I love it! Our oldest son John is retired and spends over half his year here in my mom's old 1921 home. They have pickups, and cars, and help out so we don't need any additional wheels. John is an avid fisherman and keeps fish in and out of our three larger ponds. His nieces and nephews fish to their hearts content, as does he and his mother. We are having a very dry year, and we all wonder if the water will last for our sixty big heifers, much less for our fish crop.

Even though I am not as busy on the farm as I used to be, I have not pulled out from my responsibilities in the community. As a past County Commissioner of twelve years, I still go to Court every Monday morning at 9:00 AM and support our county government. We are so lucky to have a great County Judge, Jon H. Burrows, and four dedicated County Commissioners—Richard Cortese (Precinct 1), Tim Brown (Precinct 2), Eddy Lange (Precinct 3) and John Fisher (Precinct 4).

They have an exceptional staff, particularly the judge's secretary, Peggy Dillard, and the Court's Secretary—and everyone else's—Gloria Ramos. The Court could not have picked a better pair to cover their needs. The Court works with a host of elected county officials, including the County Sheriff, County Attorney, and fine crackerjack county judges and their staffs. Our County Engineer operates under the Optional Road Law and supervises and engineers hundred of county road miles, county road crews, and all of their equipment in Bell County.

There was a day when each of the County Commissioners had their own precincts, precinct barns, and personal precinct foremen with their own road crews and equipment reporting to their commissioner. That was the situation for many, many years into the early 1980s. Then, the County Commissioners and County Judge voted in the Optional Road Law, combining all of the precinct road responsibilities into one entity under the County Engineer.

Did I mention the fact that Bell County has five District Judges, their staffs, and a District Attorney to handle the load of legal cases? The County Sheriff manages the jails and all prisoners, whether felony or misdemeanors. Felony cases are usually handled by the District Clerk, District Judge, and District Attorney. Their duties and responsibilities fall directly under state laws. The County Auditor is appointed by the District Judges and works for them in managing county monies and related activities.

It is the County Commissioner's job to provide facilities (court rooms, etc.) for the District Judges, necessary staff and their pay, plus felony jail space. Over the past few years, beginning in the 1980s, the Commissioners Court had only provided a four-court facility for district courts. But in the past few years, they have built a new legal/court complex on the outskirts of Belton. This facility houses all of the District and County Courts, their judges' offices and staff, County and District Attorneys, County and District Clerks, and a new felony jail complex. It is all completed now. The County Judge, Commissioners Court Offices, courtroom, County Treasurer, Family Courts, Auditor and staff are the only entities in the remodeled county courthouse. Our Bell County is way ahead of most counties in the State of Texas and is a model and example for all of them. I am proud to have been a part of the planning for this ultimate legal facility. I used my own four-place airplane to fly members of our County Commissioners Court and the County Judge to visit with county and state officials in California, New Mexico, Arizona, and other city/county governments, to explore the positive attributes of pursuing such a plan. Now that it is finished, Bell County can be proud of our Commissioners Court for seeing it through.

Before we came home, we had already joined the Methodist Church in Salado and the Mill Creek Golf Course—the developer and friend, Mac Sherrill, had written us to send $250 and thereby become a charter member. We were member number 59 for many years. We soon transferred our Masonic Lodge Membership to Salado number 296 and our VFW and American Legion Memberships to Belton, Texas. Our family bank was the Peoples National in Belton, which became the Compass Bank. Our "farm" bank was First in Holland and then became the First State in Salado when an old friend established the bank. In Killeen, we became very active in the Masonic Lodge, Scottish Rite Club, and Shrine Club. This gave us many contacts and friends in a hurry. We had also transferred from Fort Monmouth our membership in the National Sojourners—a group of officers who were Master Masons. We became active in their sub-group, the Heroes of '76.

Their Commander, General Harvey Jablonski, adopted us and insisted the Heroes meet at the Oliver ranch, which he named *Fort Oliver*. General Jablonski then asked me to be on his new Army Retiree Council at Fort Hood as his Air Corps Representative.

My wife Miriam has always said I am a joiner. She noted: "He belongs to everything in the community, county, state, the United States, and at Fort Hood. He has been on the Retiree Council, the Retired Officers Association, and the Military Officers Association—known as MOAA [Military Officers Association of America]. He belongs to the Army's AUSA [Association of the US Army], an association that supports and exercises political leverage for the Army and Fort Hood. Jack has welcomed and been friends with every commanding general at Fort Hood since 1980."

County Judge John Garth loved the Army but had never served. He always said he couldn't tell a general from a private, so I was his front man, to meet and greet the Fort Hood folks and keep them happy! Those Generals loved Judge Garth and paid no attention to the rank bit. In fact, eventually they and their folks maneuvered him into becoming President of their AUSA.

The Judge insisted that I run through the offices of our CTCOG (Central Texas Council of Governments), made up of seven counties. In time I was President. I was also busy with Hill Country Actions, looking after the interests of the smaller counties in our Central Texas area. All this time, I was an officer in the Lions Club, ending up as President, and President of the SAR (Sons of the American Revolution).

We continued flying our Mooney airplane to get away, enjoying weekends in El Paso, Louisiana, and so forth. After I left the county, I helped organize a Daedalian Chapter of military pilots in Killeen which continues to be active. I also organized a QB (Quiet Birdman) Hangar in Killeen, made up of old seasoned military and civilian pilots. The QB organization was formed in 1921 and has, over the years, included individuals such as Charles Lindbergh, Wiley Post, and Jimmy Doolittle. It is a great, lively organization. And last, but not least, I have joined the United Flying Octogenarians (UFO) consisting of individuals who have flown as Pilot-in-Command on or after their 80th birthday. I joined on my 82nd birthday with two years to spare. General Ben Harrison, US Army Retired of Belton, Texas, and myself, are the only two UFOs in Bell County, Texas. The UFO organization, founded in 1982 by twenty-five aviators, now boasts having more than nine hundred men and women members around the world.

There was one other aircraft pilot's organization that we organized and kept going from my days at Louisiana State University. We were called the Mississippi River *MudCats*. As mentioned previously, LSU had two *Navion* four-place Army observation planes used for ROTC cadet orientation rides. To keep the planes flying and modifications up-to-date, we flew the Navions to Lake Pontchartrain Airport at New Orleans where the Louisiana National Guard performed special maintenance. The weather never seemed favorable in Louisiana and low ceilings were common. In order to return home to Baton Rouge—usually at night—we often flew up the old Mississippi River from New Orleans to Ryan Field at Baton Rouge. We typically stayed low—some fifty feet—when we flew up the river, which was usually dimly lit with lots of night barge traffic. One night, dat rat it, before we knew it, we had flown under the tall—113 feet above water—Huey P. Long Bridge spanning the Mississippi at Baton Rouge. We then dropped over the east bank of the river into

Ryan Field. A membership certificate, complete with date and MudCat image, was later quietly presented to those accomplished River Rats!

To say that I enjoyed flying and being the pilot of any flying machine would be an understatement. I never saw an airplane I didn't like or believed I couldn't fly. The P-51 was my favorite airplane, but I also felt at home in the jet trainer, the *T-Bird* T-33. It was my home away from home. However, the Mooney M-20C stayed with me to the end! It carried me to all ends of this country, safely, for over twenty years. It took the place of the T-33. My wife Miriam was as comfortable in the Mooney as I was, and trusted it to get us home under what were sometimes terrible conditions. I could fly the Mooney in the morning and be comfortable on any one of my three farm tractors in the evening. Talk about "Full Circle": from farm mules in 1935 and earlier, to our first tractor in 1936; and from the old Interstate Aircraft trainer in 1942 to our Mooney (1980–2005). I still have my dad's full-powered Jubilee Ford tractor that he bought for $960 in 1953 with all the equipment. We now own that '53 Ford, plus a great 50-HP International Harvester diesel tractor, and a new 65-HP John Deere to do the hard work. From driving a mule to working a farm in 1935 to driving a great John Deere—with all its bells and whistles—in 2011. That is indeed "Full Circle" for an old farm boy! And to be able to return to, and own, the old Oliver farm was more than anyone could expect.

The Oliver Family
Sandra, Jack, Robert, Miriam, and John

GLOSSARY OF TERMS AND ABBREVIATIONS

313 – Public Law 313 allocated a number of civilian scientific and professional positions at salaries equivalent to that of the highest ranking Government officials. Those individuals were often referred to as *PL-313s* or simply *313s*.

AB – Airbase

ACSA – Army Communications Satellite Agency

ADC – Air Defense Command

AEC – Atomic Energy Commission

AFB – Air Force Base

AFIT – Air Force Institute of Technology

AFSC – Air Force Specialty Code

Agena – Space vehicle used in large numbers during the 1960s and 1970s as upper stage with SLV-2 *Thor*, SLV-3 *Atlas*, and SLV-5 *Titan* boosters to launch a variety of military and civilian payloads into orbit; the *Agena* itself was actually the first general-purpose satellite and formed the core for many operational satellites and experimental space vehicles.

AO – Air Officer

Atlas – The Atlas rocket; originally developed as America's first ICBM; served as basis for most American space exploration.

ATC – Air Training Command

AUSA – Association of the US Army

Bandwidth – A measure of the width of a range of frequencies

Broadband – Refers to a telecommunications signal or device of greater bandwidth, in some sense, than another standard or usual signal or device (the broader the band, the greater the capacity for traffic).

Buck Sergeant – Sergeant of the lowest rank in the military

CADF – Central Air Defense Force

CAirC – Caribbean Air Command

CIA – Central Intelligence Agency

CO – Commanding Officer

COMSAT – Communications Satellite Corporation

Crackerjack – Someone having excellent quality or ability

CRSC – Combat-Related Special Compensation

CTCOG – Central Texas Council of Governments

Dead-stick – Fly an aircraft without internal power

DCA – Defense Communications Agency

DFC – Distinguished Flying Cross

DSCS – Defense Satellite Communications System

ER – Effectiveness Report

FAA – Federal Aviation Administration

Feather – To "feather an engine" actually means to feather the propeller. The blades of the prop are pivoted in the hub so that they are parallel with the airflow, thus reducing parasite (friction) drag.

FIC – Frequency Interference Coordinator

Fish – Freshman at Texas A&M

Form 5 – Record of Air Force flying

GPS – Global Positioning System

Great War – World War I (WWI)

Green Card – Advanced instrument flying experience rating

HQ – Headquarters

HQ PACAF – Pacific Air Forces Headquarters

IG – Inspector General

III Corps – Corps of the US Army headquartered at Fort Hood, Texas; major formation of the US Army Forces Command; nickname: *Phantom Warrior.*

IP – Instructor Pilot

TF – Joint Task Force

LMSC – Lockheed Missiles and Space Company

Medevac – Medical Evacuation

MIDAS – Missile Detection and Surveillance; American military early warning satellites (18 launches)

MOAA – Military Officers Association of America

MOS – Military Occupational Specialty

NAS – Naval Air Station

NASA – National Aeronautics and Space Administration

NCO – Non-Commissioned Officer

OIC – Officer in Charge

PIO – Public Information Officer

Pisco – A brandy distilled from several different grape varieties grown in South America

PL-313 – Public Law 313 that allocated a number of civilian scientific and professional positions at salaries equivalent to that of the highest ranking Government officials. Those individuals were often referred to as *PL-313s* or simply *313s.*

PT – Physical Training

Rag-Wing – Nickname for the Stearman aircraft

R&R – Rest and Recuperation

ROTC – Reserve Officer Training Corps

SAC – Strategic Air Command

SAMOS – Satellite and Missile Observation System; American military surveillance satellites (17 launches)

SAMSO – Space and Missiles and Satellite Operations

SAR – Sons of the American Revolution

SOP – Standard Operating Procedures

TDY – Temporary Duty

TP&L – Texas Power and Light

UFO – United Flying Octogenarians

UN – United Nations

USAF – United States Air Force

VA – Veterans Administration

Wash out – Elimination from training

WDD – Western Development Division; established in 1954 under the command of Brig Gen Bernard A. Schriever

WDL – Western Development Laboratories

Wideband – A relative term used to describe a wide range of frequencies in a spectrum.

GLOSSARY OF US MILITARY RANKS

1LT – First Lieutenant (Army)

1st Lt – First Lieutenant (Air Force)

2d Lt – Second Lieutenant (Air Force)

2nd LT – Second Lieutenant (Air Force O-1)

2LT – Second Lieutenant (Army)

1SG – First Sergeant (Army E-8)

1SGT – First Sergeant (Air Force E-8)

AB – Airman Basic (Air Force E-1)

A1C – Airman 1st Class (Air Force E-3)

BG – Brigadier General (1-Star) (Army O-7)

Brig Gen – Brigadier General (1-Star) (Air Force O-7)

BRIG GEN – Brigadier General (1-Star) (Air Force O-7)

Buck Sergeant – Sergeant of the lowest rank in the military

CMSgt – Chief Master Sergeant (Air Force E-9; highest AF enlisted rank)

CMSAF – Chief Master Sergeant of the Air Force (Air Force E-9 – Senior Enlisted Member)

COL – Colonel (Air Force and Army O-6)

CPL – Corporal (Army and Marines E-4)

CPT – Captain

CSM – Command Sergeant Major (Army E9; highest Army enlisted rank)

Gen – General (4-Star) (Air Force)

GEN – General (4-Star) (Army)

LT – Lieutenant

LTC – Lieutenant Colonel (Army)

Lt Col – Lieutenant Colonel (Air Force)

LT COL – Lieutenant Colonel (Air Force O-5)

LTG – Lieutenant General (3-Star) (Army)

Lt Gen – Lieutenant General (3-Star) (Air Force)

MAJ – Major (O-4) – (Air Force, Army)

MG – Major General (2-Star) (Army O-8)

Maj Gen – *Major General (2-Star) (Air Force and Marines O-8)*

MAJ GEN – Major General (2-Star) (Air Force and Marines O-8)

MSgt – Master Sergeant (Air Force E-7)

MSGT – Master Sergeant (Air Force E-7)

PFC – Private First Class (US Military)

PV2 – Private 2nd class (Army E-2)

PVT – Private (Army and Marines E-1)

SFC – Sergeant First Class (Army E7)

SGM – Sergeant Major (Army E9; sometimes referred to as Staff Sergeant Major)

Sgt – Sergeant (Marines)

SGT – Sergeant (Army E5)

SMA – Sergeant Major of the Army (Army E9; Senior Enlisted Member)

SMSgt – Senior Master Sergeant (Air Force E-8)

SMSGT – Senior Master Sergeant (Air Force E-8)

SPC – Specialist (Army E-4)

SrA – Senior Airman (Air Force E-4)

SSG – Staff Sergeant (Army E-6)

SSgt – Staff Sergeant (Air Force E-5; Marines E-6)

SSGT – Staff Sergeant (Air Force E-5)

TSgt – Technical Sergeant (Air Force E-6)

TSGT – Technical Sergeant (Air Force E-6)

Made in the USA
San Bernardino, CA
15 October 2015